SCENARIO-BASED STRATEGIC PLANNING

Roland Berger
School of Strategy and Economics

BURKHARD SCHWENKER · TORSTEN WULF

SCENARIO-BASED STRATEGIC PLANNING

Developing Strategies in an Uncertain World

SERIES EDITORS

DR. KATRIN VERNAU
Partner
Roland Berger Strategy Consultants
Dean
Roland Berger School
of Strategy and Economics

KLAUS FUEST
Principal
Roland Berger Strategy Consultants
Roland Berger School
of Strategy and Economics

DR. CHRISTIAN KRYS
Senior Expert
Roland Berger Strategy Consultants
Roland Berger School
of Strategy and Economics

EDITORS

PROF. DR. BURKHARD SCHWENKER
CEO
Roland Berger Strategy Consultants
Chairman
Roland Berger School
of Strategy and Economics
Academic Director
HHL Center for Strategy and Scenario Planning

PROF. DR. TORSTEN WULF
Professor of Strategic and International Management
Philipps-Universität Marburg
Academic Director
HHL Center for Strategy and Scenario Planning

ISBN 978-3-658-04214-1   ISBN 978-3-658-02875-6 (eBook)
DOI 10.1007/ 978-3-658-02875-6

Die Deutsche Nationalbibliothek verzeichnet diese Publikation in der Deutschen Nationalbibliografie; detaillierte bibliografische Daten sind im Internet über http://dnb.d-nb.de abrufbar.

Springer Gabler
© Springer Fachmedien Wiesbaden 2013
Softcover re-print of the Hardcover 1st edition 2013
Das Werk einschließlich aller seiner Teile ist urheberrechtlich geschützt. Jede Verwertung, die nicht ausdrücklich vom Urheberrechtsgesetz zugelassen ist, bedarf der vorherigen Zustimmung des Verlags. Das gilt insbesondere für Vervielfältigungen, Bearbeitungen, Übersetzungen, Mikroverfilmungen und die Einspeicherung und Verarbeitung in elektronischen Systemen.

Die Wiedergabe von Gebrauchsnamen, Handelsnamen, Warenbezeichnungen usw. in diesem Werk berechtigt auch ohne besondere Kennzeichnung nicht zu der Annahme, dass solche Namen im Sinne der Warenzeichen und Markenschutz-Gesetzgebung als frei zu betrachten wären und daher von jedermann benutzt werden dürften.

Lektorat: Stefanie A. Winter
Layout und Satz: workformedia | Frankfurt am Main | München

Gedruckt auf säurefreiem und chlorfrei gebleichtem Papier

Springer Gabler ist eine Marke von Springer DE. Springer DE ist Teil der Fachverlagsgruppe Springer Science+Business Media
www.springer-gabler.de

"LET OUR ADVANCE WORRYING
BECOME ADVANCE THINKING
AND PLANNING."
WINSTON CHURCHILL

CONTENTS

CHAPTER 1

INTRODUCTION   11
1.1   An uncertain world   12
1.2   Scenario-based strategic planning   14
1.3   The goal of this book   15
1.4   References   17

CHAPTER 2

THE CHALLENGES OF STRATEGIC MANAGEMENT
IN THE TWENTY-FIRST CENTURY   21
2.1   Determinants of environmental uncertainty   22
2.2   The evolution of strategic planning   30
2.3   Techniques of predicting the future   36
2.4   Conclusions   38
2.5   References   38

CHAPTER 3

SCENARIO-BASED STRATEGIC PLANNING:
A NEW APPROACH TO COPING WITH UNCERTAINTY   43
3.1   Introduction   44
3.2   Scenario planning – the basis for modern strategic planning   46
3.3   Designing a scenario-based approach to strategic planning   49
3.4   Conclusion   64
3.5   References   64

CHAPTER 4

SIX TOOLS FOR SCENARIO-BASED STRATEGIC PLANNING
AND THEIR APPLICATION   69
4.1   Introducing tools one and two:
       The framing checklist and 360° stakeholder feedback   70
4.2   Applying frameworks one and two: The framing checklist
       and 360° stakeholder feedback in the European airline industry   88

4.3 Introducing tools three and four: The impact/uncertainty grid and the scenario matrix   96
4.4 Applying frameworks three and four: The impact/uncertainty grid and the scenario matrix in the European airline industry   112
4.5 Introducing tools five and six:
    The strategy manual and the monitoring cockpit   130
4.6 Applying frameworks five and six: The strategy manual and the scenario cockpit in the European airline industry   144

CHAPTER 5
SCENARIO-BASED STRATEGIC PLANNING –
USING SCENARIO PLANNING TO IDENTIFY OPPORTUNITIES
IN A MULTI-SECTOR INDUSTRY   155
5.1 Introduction   156
5.2 Challenge and objectives   157
5.3 Methodology/Approach   157
5.4 Best practices   171
5.5 Conclusions   172

CHAPTER 6
THE BENEFITS OF SCENARIO-BASED PLANNING –
HOW SCENARIO-BASED STRATEGIC PLANNING AFFECTS
THE BEHAVIOR OF MANAGERS   175
6.1 Introduction   176
6.2 Decision-making comprehensiveness and speed   179
6.3 Cognitive biases   182
6.4 An integrative model of decision quality   185
6.5 Scenario-based strategic planning   186
6.6 Conclusion   190
6.7 References   191

CHAPTER 7
THE BENEFITS OF SCENARIO-BASED PLANNING – HOW SCENARIO-BASED PLANNING FOSTERS FLEXIBLE STRATEGIES   197
7.1 Introduction   198
7.2 Strategic flexibility – Opening the door to a change of strategy   199

7.3 Obstacles to strategic flexibility   202
7.4 Practical application   204
7.5 Scenario-based planning as a tool to craft strategic flexibility   207
7.6 References   210

CHAPTER 8

CONCLUSION – GOOD MANAGEMENT AND SCENARIO PLANNING   215
8.1 The challenges of good management today   216
8.2 How scenario planning supports good management in uncertain times   218
8.3 References   220

Table of Figures   223
About the Editors, Authors and RBSE   226

1. Introduction

BURKHARD SCHWENKER, TORSTEN WULF

In an increasingly uncertain world characterized by complexity and volatility, managers must be more flexible in their strategy processes. Traditional strategic management frameworks fail to provide adequate answers in this context. Our solution is "scenario-based strategic planning", a framework for strategic management in an uncertain world. In this chapter, we introduce this approach and outline the structure of the book.

1.1 AN UNCERTAIN WORLD

The 2008 financial crisis and near-default of Greece, leading to political discussions about the future of the Eurozone, indicate clearly the extent to which management today is influenced by what is happening in the general environment. The modern business world is plagued by uncertainty. It is far more complex and volatile than 30 years ago. Planning has become more difficult. Key factors change quickly and have a major impact around the globe.

The 2008 financial crisis was unprecedented in terms of its magnitude, resulting in a decline of global GDP in 2009. However, economic disruptions of one sort or another are far more common now than in the past. A study by Bordo et al. (2001) shows that the frequency of major crises has doubled since the oil crisis of the 1970s. Economic volatility is also seen on an industry level. Product lifecycles are shortening and customer demands changing more rapidly. This leaves managers with less time to make decisions and requires greater flexibility in business systems.

Globalization has made the world more interconnected. New technology and free trade between the major economic zones have increased global growth and wealth, but they have also made management and operations more complex for organizations (Schwenker/Boetzel, 2007). This complexity, combined with the increasing volatility of industries and the general environment, adds to the levels of uncertainty in the business world. It creates new challenges for management and strategic decision-making, as future developments are less predictable than in the past.

Under these circumstances, traditional planning tools such as Porter's Five Forces or the market share-growth matrix are less and less able to meet the demands of executives and strategic planners. A major reason is that they originated in the 1960s and 1970s in a less complex and volatile world (Ansoff, 1957; Porter, 1979; Porter, 1980). Most traditional frameworks do not account for volatility. They rather provide static analyses of the current situation and lack a dynamic element that considers developments over time. Furthermore, they are generally based on the assumption of constant growth and build their normative strategic recommendations around this assumption. As we can see today, in many industries that assumption is simply no longer tenable.

Since the 1990s, traditional approaches to strategic planning and their underlying concepts have attracted considerable criticism from both researchers and practitioners (Mintzberg 1991; Mintzberg, 1994a; Prahalad and Hamel, 1994; Dye, Sibony and Viguerie, 2009). Criticism relates particularly to the core tenet of strategic planning that plans should be developed for a single future direction. Many analysts argue that the traditional concepts and frameworks of strategic planning do not meet the requirements of successful planning in a dynamic, complex and increasingly volatile business environment (Camillus/Datta, 1991; Eisenhardt/Sull, 2001; Grant, 2003).

In light of these challenges, strategic managers in today's business environment have to find answers to two key questions:
1. How can we incorporate volatility, complexity and uncertainty that we observe in many industries today into strategic planning?
2. How can we make strategies more flexible and adaptive to changing environments?

This book is an attempt to answer these questions. At the heart of the book lies the introduction of what we call "scenario-based strategic planning", a methodological framework for creating strategies in an uncertain world.

Scenario planning originated in the 1970s at the oil company Shell (Wack, 1985). It differs from earlier strategy frameworks in that it integrates uncertainty into the strategy process, taking into consideration volatility and complexity. In particular, it analyzes different possible future developments and incorporates factors both from the industry under examination and the general environment into its framework. Moreover, by developing different strategic options, it provides a flexibility that allows companies to adapt to volatility in their environment.

However, the disadvantage of most scenario planning approaches – those of van der Heijden (2005) or Schoemaker (1995), say – is that they are complicated to apply in practice. Indeed, the amount of time and effort required puts many companies off. This is where our new approach to scenario-based strategic planning comes in. Its main advantage lies in the ease of its application thanks to its tool-based design. The approach was developed as part of a joint project between Roland Berger Strategy Consultants and HHL Leipzig Graduate School of Management to find ways to better use scenario planning in corporate practice.

1.2
SCENARIO-BASED STRATEGIC PLANNING

The HHL-Roland Berger approach to scenario-based strategic planning is an innovative framework based on six continuous process steps. These steps incorporate most of what traditional approaches do, in a structured, comprehensive process. More importantly, our approach supports each of these six process steps with a specific tool. These tools help managers apply the framework easily and consistently over time. This book describes the six steps and their supporting tools in depth, enabling business people and students to implement the approach directly and apply it to the specific strategic challenges faced by different industries (Wulf et al., 2011; Wulf et al., 2012).

The tools for each of the six process steps make developing flexible strategies based on scenarios significantly quicker than more traditional scenario-based approaches. In our experience, companies can apply our approach in just four to six weeks, compared to the five months to a year typically needed for traditional approaches (Bradfield, 2008; Moyer, 1996; Shell International, 2003). The shorter timeframe is more in line with the amount of time normally available for strategic planning in businesses (Grant, 2003; Ocasio/Joseph, 2008).

Because it is easy to apply, our approach can be used for shorter planning periods. Traditionally, companies use scenario planning for long-term planning only, with time horizons of 15 to 20 years (van der Heijden, 2005). Traditional scenario planning is not suitable for planning periods under five years due its complexity. Our approach, in contrast, is applicable for such planning horizons and therefore lays the foundations for integrating scenario planning into the strategic planning process.

The HHL-Roland Berger approach to scenario-based strategic planning builds on traditional scenario planning techniques and offers all the benefits that they provide. It takes into consideration a variety of factors from inside and outside the organization to account for complexity, and it develops multiple scenarios and strategic options to counteract volatility. In addition, it gives organizations greater strategic flexibility by providing them with different strategy options. These options are developed as part of the process and can be implemented depending on what happens in the general environment. In addition, the approach can be applied very quickly in practice, which makes it suitable for shorter planning periods than is possible with traditional strategic planning methods.

1.3
THE GOAL OF THIS BOOK

This book aims to show managers how it is possible to create robust strategies in today's increasingly uncertain business environment. However volatile or complex the environment, companies still need to take investment decisions and develop strategies. In this book, we tackle the challenges that this presents. Our target audience is both business executives and students of management.

A large part of this book is dedicated to describing the HHL-Roland Berger approach to scenario-based strategic planning. We include detailed descriptions of each of the six process steps and their supporting tools, as well as examples of their application in corporate practice.

The book has three main messages that we believe are central for managers operating in an uncertain world:

SCENARIO-BASED STRATEGIC PLANNING

1. Managers need to understand the fundamental impact of uncertainty on planning and decision making, as well as its consequences for strategic management in general.
2. Scenario-based planning provides a powerful methodological framework to account for uncertainty, volatility and complexity in the strategic management process.
3. Scenario planning can increase the quality of strategic decisions in uncertain environments and lead to flexible strategies that can counteract volatility.

These three messages underlie the structure of the book. Each of the book's chapters focuses on one message and presents the reasoning behind it in greater depth. Following this introductory section, the second chapter looks at the core challenges facing strategic management in the twenty-first century. Cornelia Geißler and Christian Krys identify uncertainty as a major issue and analyze its main determinants: volatility, complexity and ambiguity. Based on many examples, the authors show how much more uncertain the world has become for managers today. They take a close look at traditional planning tools and point out their merits and limitations. Finally, they discuss different forecasting methodologies such as prediction markets or simulations that can be used to reduce uncertainty and assess the impact of potential changes.

The third chapter gives an overview of the HHL-Roland Berger approach to scenario-based strategic planning as well as the underlying concepts and ideas. Torsten Wulf, Philip Meißner, Christian Brands and Stephan Stubner describe the overall methodology and its benefits for the strategic management process. They also show how the approach can be integrated into a company's strategic planning process. In the fourth chapter, Torsten Wulf, Christian Brands and Philip Meißner present each of the six tools used as part of the approach in detail. They also demonstrate how each tool is applied in practice based on a case study from the European airline industry. In the fifth chapter, Nicklas Holgersson and Duce Gotora show how scenario-based strategic planning can be applied in a consulting project taking one of the world's largest multi-sector companies as an example.

The sixth chapter discusses the benefits of scenario-based strategic planning for strategic decision making. Philip Meißner analyzes the approach's potential for improving decision quality in the management process. He finds that scenario planning can increase comprehensiveness as well as speed, and reduce the negative effects of cognitive biases, all of which have been shown to increase decision quality. He concludes that, thanks to its positive influence on the quality of decisions, scenario planning is also likely to positively affect performance. In the seventh chapter Cornelia Geißler and Christian Krys address a second benefit of scenario-based strategic planning. They emphasize the importance of strategic flexibility and identify potential obstacles that prevent companies from achieving this capability. Finally, they analyze the influence of scenario planning on flexibility. The final chapter presents an outlook on how strategic management will evolve in the coming years and decades.

This book aims to bridge the gap between research and practice. It offers an application-oriented approach that is strongly rooted in academic research. The different case studies aim to demonstrate the relevance of scenario-based planning for the business community and show how the approach can be implemented in organizations.

Stretching the imagination and "thinking outside the box" is a crucial part of scenario planning. We hope that this book achieves this goal and helps change the way you think about strategic management.

1.4
REFERENCES

Ansoff HI. 1957. Strategies for Diversification. *Harvard Business Review* 35(5): 113-124.

Bordo M., Eichengreen B., Klingebiel D., Martinez-Peria M. 2001. Is the Crisis Problem Growing More Severe? *Economic Policy* 16(32): 51-82.

Bradfield RM. 2008. Cognitive Barriers in the Scenario Development Process. *Advances in Developing Human Resources* 10(2): 198-215.

Camillus JC., Datta DK. 1991 Managing strategic issues in a turbulent environment. *Long Range Planning* 24(2): 67-74.

Dye R., Sibony O., Viguerie P. 2009. Strategic planning: Three tips for 2009. *The McKinsey Quarterly* 9(1): 1-2.

Eisenhardt KM., Sull DN. 2001. Strategy as Simple Rules. *Harvard Business Review* 79(1): 106-116.

Grant RM. 2003. Strategic Planning in a Turbulent Environment: Evidence from the Oil Majors. *Strategic Management Journal* 24(6): 491-517.

Mintzberg H. 1991. Learning 1, planning 0: reply to Igor Ansoff. *Strategic Management Journal* 12(6): 463-466.

Mintzberg H. 1994a. *The Rise and Fall of Strategic Planning*. New York: The Free Press.

Moyer K. 1996. Scenario Planning at British Airways-A Case Study. *Long Range Planning* 29(2): 172-181.

Ocasio W., Joseph J. 2008. Rise and Fall- or Transformation? The Evolution of Strategic Planning at the General Electric Company 1940-2006. *Long Range Planning* 41(3): 248-272.

Porter ME. 1979. How Competitive Forces Shape Strategy. *Harvard Business Review* 57(2): 137-145.

Porter ME. 1980. *Competitive Advantage: Techniques for analyzing Industries and Competitors*. New York: The Free Press.

Prahalad CK., Hamel G. 1994. *Competing for the future*. Boston: Harvard Business School Press.

Schoemaker P. 1995. Scenario Planning: A Tool for Strategic Thinking. *Sloan Management Review* 37(2): 25-40.

Schwenker B., Boetzel S. 2007. *Making Growth Work – How Companies Can Expand and Become More Efficient*. Berlin: Springer.

Shell International 2003. *Scenarios: An Explorer's Guide*. London: Shell.

van der Heijden K. 2005. *Scenarios: The Art of Strategic Conversation*. Chichester: John Wiley & Sons.

Wack P. 1985. Scenarios: Uncharted waters ahead. *Harvard Business Review* 63(5): 73-89.

Wulf T., Meißner P., Stubner S. 2010. Szenario-basierte strategische Planung – ein Ansatz zur Integration der Szenarioplanung in die strategische Planung, in: Gausemeier, J. (Hrsg.): *Vorausschau und Technologieplanung*, Paderborn, 443 – 458.

Wulf T., Stubner S., Meißner P., Brands C. (2012) Szenariobasierte strategische Planung in volatilen Umfeldern. *Zeitschrift* für Controlling & Management special issue 2/2012: 34-38.

2. The challenges of strategic management in the twenty-first century

CORNELIA GEISSLER, CHRISTIAN KRYS

Markets around the globe are set to experience increasing turbulence in the coming years. That means greater uncertainty for companies' strategic planning – more volatility, more complexity and more ambiguity. The tools managers use for strategic planning and forecasting have changed considerably in the past few decades. But they are inadequate when faced with today's fast-changing environments. Scenario-based planning can be the answer to cope with the challenges of today's business.

2.1 DETERMINANTS OF ENVIRONMENTAL UNCERTAINTY

Economic forecasters use complex models to help them understand economic change. But trends are unreliable and future developments often far from clear.

Uncertainty is an entrepreneur's everyday business. It can be understood as an individual's inability to predict something accurately (Miliken, 1987). In the business world, managers have to deal with different kinds of uncertainty. They face uncertainty in the overall environment – the macroeconomic, political, social, technological and environmental framework in which they operate. They also face uncertainty in their specific industry. Another way of categorization is to differentiate between uncertainty about the actual state, uncertainty about effects and impacts, and uncertainty about responses or adequate measures (Miliken, 1987).

As early as 1848, the revolutionary socialists Karl Marx and Friedrich Engels wrote in the Communist Manifesto that the "constant revolutionizing of production, uninterrupted disturbance of all social conditions, everlasting uncertainty and agitation" distinguished the current time from earlier periods (Marx/Engels, 1969).

Underestimating this uncertainty can be hazardous. At worst, it leads to strategies that are unable to protect the company against threats. At best, it leads to strategies that ignore the potential opportunities inherent in uncertainty.

Let's look at some historical examples. These examples show how significant the long-term consequences of uncertainty – and decisions based on uncertainty – can be. Back in 1876, the financial services company Western Union believed that the telephone would never replace the telegraph. An internal memo from that year stated that "the telephone has too many shortcomings to be seriously considered as a means of communication." Today, the number of cell phone subscriptions alone is about six billion (ITU, 2012).

Another example: In 1977, Kenneth H. Olsen, then president of the American IT firm Digital Equipment Corporation, is said to have announced that "there is no reason for any individual to have a computer in their home." At that time, the explosion in the personal computer market could not be foreseen with any clarity, but it was certainly one of the possibilities that industry experts were discussing. Nowadays we have more than 1.6 billon personal computer users around the globe (Gartner Group, 2010).

Further examples of glaring misjudgments (Incorrect predictions, 2013) include the legendary quote by Darryl Zanuck, movie producer at 20th Century Fox, who stated in 1946 that "television won't last, because people will soon get tired of staring at a plywood box every night." French Marshall Ferdinand Foch, a famous military theorist and supreme commander of the Allied armies in the closing year of World War I, said in 1911: "Airplanes are interesting toys, but of no military value." Similarly, Germany's last Kaiser, Wilhelm II, failed to grasp the huge potential of cars when he stated in 1905 (Wüst, 2006): "I believe in horses. Automobiles are a passing phenomenon."

The list of such quotes could go on indefinitely. Yet even these few examples make the point with abundant clarity: Cling rigidly to your dogmas and doctrines and you will never find the right answers in a world of uncertainty where change is as dynamic as it is profound. Tread the beaten path, think the way you have always thought – and you will quite simply be swept away by new developments.

This principle has never been more true than in the day in which we live. Today, the pace of environmental change has accelerated significantly. More than ever before, tools are needed to handle uncertainty. Of course, uncertainty cannot be reduced to zero. But decision makers need reliable guidelines and facts on which to base their strategic planning and investments. How, then, can managers develop a sustainable strategy in fast-changing environments? How can they overcome – or at least embrace – uncertainty in their decision-making processes?

Below, we look in turn at what we consider the three core dimensions of uncertainty – volatility, complexity and ambiguity.

2.1.1
VOLATILITY

How do environmental parameters react to impulses that are hard to predict? Volatility comprises both what we call "firm-level volatility" and "aggregate volatility". The two types of volatility are, of course, interrelated – as we saw during the financial crisis of 2008.

"Firm-level volatility" involves changes in a company's workforce, sales, earnings, capital expenditure or the price of raw materials (Comin/Philippon, 2006).

Strategic decisions are strongly influenced by sudden changes that affect a company's individual situation. One example of such firm-level volatility is the major shifts in the price of the raw materials copper, platinum and nickel seen in recent years (see Figure 2-1). These materials are required by specific industries; their price has become a strategically relevant parameter. In addition, shorter product lifecycles and rapidly changing technology also make long-term decisions difficult, often leading to expensive strategies based on trial and error.

The fast spread of new technology also causes volatility. Thus, it took radio 38 years to reach 50 million people, whereas the social network Facebook achieved the same feat in less than two years. Similarly, mobile-only Internet users (users with no fixed broadband) numbered just 14 million in 2010, but they are expected to grow 34% a year to 2030, from under 1% of the world's population to around 60% (Roland Berger Strategy Consultants, 2011).

FIGURE 2.1: SELECTED METAL PRICES, 2000-2013
[INDEX, END OF JAN 2000 = 100]

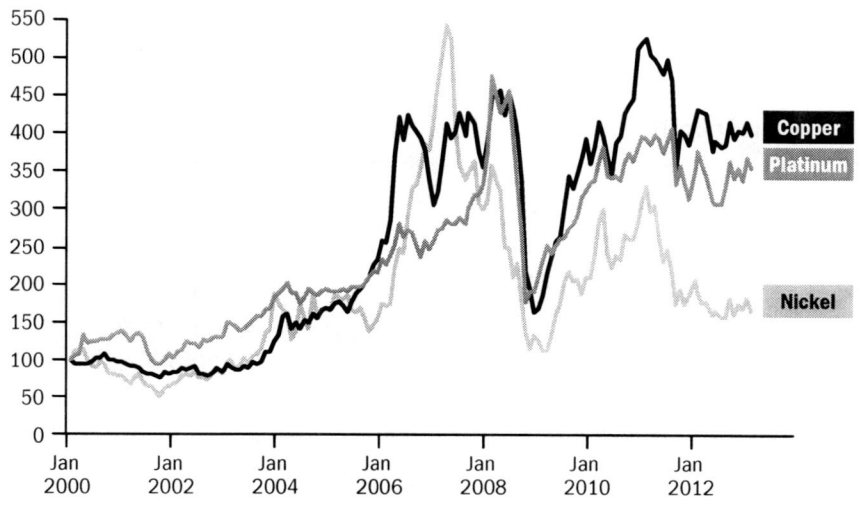

Source: Bloomberg, Roland Berger calculation

"Aggregate volatility" refers to fast, large-scale changes in macro-indicators such as GDP growth on a national, regional or global level. It can result from having strongly interconnected sectors. "The recent economic crisis has further highlighted the importance of interconnections between firms and sectors in the economy. Both the spread of the risks emanating from the so-called 'toxic' assets on the balance sheets of several financial institutions to the rest of the financial sector, and the transmission of the economic problems of the financial sector to the rest of the economy have been linked to such interconnections. In addition, government policies aimed at shoring up several key financial institutions and the assistance to General Motors and Chrysler in the midst of the crisis were both justified, not so much because these institutions were 'too big to fail', but because they were 'too interconnected to fail'"(Acemoglu et al., 2010, p. 1).

The fact that aggregate volatility is very great indeed in the present day can be seen from other telling examples. In response to the reactor disaster in Fukushima, the Merkel government resolved a *volte-face* in Germany's energy policy that, in a very short space of time, has radically altered the planning parameters for the energy sector and for German industry as a whole. The resultant expedited switch from nuclear energy and fossil fuels to renewable energy necessitates completely new transitional structures and energy storage options and even reopens the debate about the affordability of electricity.

Meanwhile, the USA is using "fracking" and horizontal drilling techniques to tap oil and gas reserves that were hitherto difficult to access. By reducing energy consumption – in particular car fuel consumption – at the same time, it is thus increasingly breaking free of its dependence on energy imports from the Middle East. Thus, while all past forecasts have seen it as a major energy importer, the USA is now poised to become a net gas exporter as of 2020 and a net oil exporter as of 2035 (IEA, 2012). That will do more than simply make US industry more competitive: One dramatic outcome could be that the country's geopolitical interest in the Middle East might wane. What consequences *that* could have for the region is, from a present perspective, utterly imponderable. Clearly, realities that once appeared to be cast in stone can change quickly and fundamentally in today's volatile world. And that has far-reaching consequences in so many different areas.

2.1.2
COMPLEXITY

What factors must managers take into account when formulating strategies? In most organizations today, major change is the rule rather than the exception. Shifts in leadership, overseas initiatives, new products and services all cause unpredictability. Snowden and Boone identify the following features of complex systems (Snowden/Boone, 2007):
- The elements are connected and interacting
- Minor impacts can produce disproportionately major consequences
- The whole is greater than the sum of its inputs and assets

- Hindsight does not lead to helpful implications for the future as external conditions are constantly changing
- Agents and the system constrain one another

Complexity results from companies having to navigate a growing number of dimensions when developing strategy. Network effects and change on different levels lead to even greater complexity. The factors involved are often interrelated, making the task particularly challenging. Below, we give some examples of how complexity impacts the everyday business of management: the broader range of stakeholder interests, increasing global presence, variety of products and information overload.

BROADER RANGE OF STAKEHOLDER INTERESTS

Today's companies need to address a broader range of stakeholder interests than in the past. Governments, activists and the media have become adept at holding companies to account for the social consequences of their activities. Corporate social responsibility (CSR) has emerged as a key priority for business leaders around the world, affecting such diverse areas as the management of supply chains, corporate governance and intercultural leadership. For example, tobacco firms have had to defend themselves for causing lung cancer. Pharmaceutical companies found that they were expected to respond to the AIDS pandemic in Africa, even though it had little to do with their primary products and markets. Fast-food and packaged food companies are being held responsible for obesity and poor nutrition (Porter, 2006). The tradeoffs that become necessary make it very difficult to identify a single strategy that will be effective in every situation.

INCREASING GLOBAL PRESENCE

Globalization is very real in everyday life. Who would have thought that Chinese brands would ever make it to Hollywood? Yet the latest "Transformers" movie is full of product placements for Chinese firms. Many companies, especially in the industrialized and emerging countries, make a big portion of their total revenues and profits through foreign sales. "... about 40% of profit for firms listed in the S&P 500 stock index [is] now coming from overseas" (Newman, 2011). And this is only the beginning: worldwide, just 10% of fixed investments go to foreign countries

(Ghemawat 2011). Globalization will further increase in the coming decades. Exports and foreign direct investments will grow significantly faster than GDP as companies are supplying goods and services to an ever wider range of international markets. They have to take into account many different factors in their strategic planning. For example, new local markets require research into target groups, purchasing patterns, regulatory frameworks and currency risks.

VARIETY OF PRODUCTS

Buyers today are used to a wide range of choices. The complexity of product portfolios contributes to the many challenges facing strategic planning. This is true especially for the consumer markets. At the beginning of the twentieth century, Henry Ford famously stated that his customers could have a car painted any color they wanted – so long as it was black. Today, buyers can choose from a wide range of specifications, from the textiles for the seat covers to the size of the engine. Hundreds of different parts means millions of different product permutations. Companies constantly launch new products and line extensions. With added complexity, the cost of managing that complexity multiplies and margins shrink. The complexity that began in the product line spreads outward through every facet of the company's operations, including the supply chain, availability of spare parts and innovation activities.

INFORMATION OVERLOAD

Information overload is an old problem, but the speed with which the sheer volume of available information is growing is new. With the internet and even faster data transfer all over the globe any amount of information can be exchanged in real time. The amount of data stored now doubles every 18 months (Roland Berger Strategy Consultants, 2011). Digital information is generated by a wide range of sensors, instruments and simulations. Companies find themselves unable to organize, analyze and store it quickly enough. Data is also increasingly fragmented. Managers are constantly bombarded with unrelated bits and pieces of data – a comment from a friend one moment, information on the consequences of the Euro crisis the next. With the information floodgates well and truly open, content engulfs us in countless different formats, from text messages and tweets to Facebook messages and voicemail. Current research suggests that this growing volume of information can have a negative effect on decision making, innovation capacity and productivity (Hemp, 2009).

2.1.3
AMBIGUITY

How accurately can we predict the impact of management initiatives on a company's performance? Decision making is complicated by the fact that it is often not clear which variables are involved and what their precise role is. Managers are facing complex situations that have never occurred before. Take the eurozone crisis. It is not clear in which way political short time measures will impact the mid-term and long-term environments of entrepreneurial decisions. It seems that for example Ireland takes a different development than Spain and Greece. Ambiguity means a lack of clarity (Schrader et al., 1993). Strategic decisions are risky because decision makers lack potentially important information and are therefore uncertain about the probability of forthcoming events. "Causal ambiguity" is also a factor here – the uncertainty that derives from unclear causal connections between actions and results (Lippmann/Rumelt, 1982).

Lack of knowledge about the relationships between actions and results is an everyday reality for managers working in unstable environments. Even where they can identify and monitor weak signals, it is not easy for them to interpret these signals correctly. An example: The percentage of households in China owning a car is rising. But what does that mean for future business models? Will Western companies profit in the long term? Or will it be the Chinese automotive industry that benefits most?

We have seen that managers today face more volatility, more complexity and more ambiguity than they did in the past. So, are the existing approaches and tools of strategic planning and the current methods of predicting the future able to cope with these new challenges? To answer that question we will have a closer look to these approaches, tools and techniques.

2.2
THE EVOLUTION OF STRATEGIC PLANNING

Whoever wants to set up an effective process of strategic planning needs to understand how organizations and their specific situation interact with the overall environment. Therefore it is useful to observe the development of different solutions over time. The idea of strategic planning as a specific task for the organization – often separated into its own organizational unit – first emerged in the 1950s. Large American and European companies began formulating strategies for individual business units and coordinating these strategies with each other. Researchers and practitioners such as Igor Ansoff, Bruce Henderson and Alfred Chandler greatly influenced the emerging field. Popular frameworks included the product/market grid, the SWOT analysis and the BCG matrix. These iconic methods influenced not only strategic planning but spread to other areas of business, too.

The following decades saw many changes in strategic planning. From a two-dimensional exercise, it developed into a more holistic approach. Below, we briefly chart the history of the field, looking at the (to some extent overlapping) periods of what we call the "golden age", the strategic process era and the multi-perspective view.

2.2.1
THE GOLDEN AGE OF STRATEGIC PLANNING

Business managers and academics first became interested in strategic planning in the 1960s. New institutions were founded to deal with the approach: in the United States, the American Society of Corporate Planners (1961) was founded, later merging with the Planning Executives Institute to create the Planning Forum (eventually renamed the Strategic Leadership Forum). In the United Kingdom, the Long Range Planning Society was founded in 1966 and later renamed the Strategic Planning Society (Grant, 2003). The most important tools and methods developed in the golden age of strategic planning are described below.

◆ **Ansoff's strategic choices for growth**: Mathematician and professor of management Igor Ansoff developed the first method for measuring the profit potential of alternative product-market strategies. His approach begins by forecasting trends and contingencies and then works toward the company's needs and long-term objectives (Ansoff, 1957). Ansoff gives four basic options for strategic moves: market penetration, diversification, product development and brand development. Each of these is positioned on a product-market-map. He also proposes making growth forecasts by observing political and economic trends as well as industry trends and manufacturing costs.

- **SWOT analysis**: SWOT (strengths-weaknesses-opportunities-threats) analysis is a way of looking at a company's strategic position in the market. Its origins lie in the work of business policy experts at the Harvard Business School and other American business schools from the 1960s onwards. Thus, Kenneth Andrews (Andrews, 1971) claims that good strategy means ensuring a fit between the external situation faced by a firm (its threats and opportunities) and its own internal qualities or characteristics (its strengths and weaknesses).
- **BCG portfolio matrix**: The BCG portfolio matrix helps companies find growth fields in their product lines. The tool was developed for Boston Consulting Group by Bruce Henderson in the 1960s. Products are mapped in terms of market growth and relative market share. On this basis, they are classified as "dogs", "cash cows", "stars" or "question marks". The BCG matrix is based on two ideas: the "product lifecycle curve" and the "learning curve". The product lifecycle curve captures the idea that products go through different stages from launch to decline. The learning curve expresses the relationship between experience and efficiency: the more often a task is performed, the lower the cost of doing it.
- **Porter's five forces analysis**: Porter sees the corporate strategist's job as understanding and coping with competition. His analytical model makes it possible to assess the nature of competition in an industry. It looks not just at established industry rivals, but at four further competitive forces: customers, suppliers, potential entrants, and substitute products (Porter, 2008). The rivalry that results from all five forces defines an industry's structure and shapes the nature of competitive interaction within it. The five forces thus determine industry attractiveness and long-term industry profitability.

Research into strategic management was revolutionized by the emergence of large commercial databases such as PIMS (Profit Impact of Market Strategy) and

Compustat. Researchers also carried out large-scale surveys and detailed studies of archival sources. Many studies explore the impact of strategic planning on company performance. However, disagreement remains about which aspects of strategic planning influence company performance positively, and how. Indeed, the research has been unable to find a clear correlation between strategic planning and better performance.

The aforementioned approaches of strategic planning have their strong merits and are partly still used today. Nevertheless they also have clear disadvantages in an uncertain world. Taking a deterministic worldview works only in relatively stable environments, where existing conditions are preserved and only incremental change is allowed. In addition, early versions of strategic planning tried to formulate a single, ideal strategy – one that would perform better than all others. As environments began changing faster, these ideal strategies simply didn't deliver. The lack of macroeconomic stability, exchange rate volatility, the microelectronics revolution and the emergence of newly industrializing countries marked the end of postwar economic stability (Grant, 2003). Faced with unreliable prognoses and new competitive landscapes, the "ideal strategy" soon became obsolete. Traditional strategic planning was replaced by the approach of the strategic process.

2.2.2
THE STRATEGIC PROCESS ERA

Inspired by Henry Mintzberg, strategists argued that social reality is not a constant. Moreover, strategists are part of the system and therefore cannot judge a situation objectively (Mintzberg, 1994). Certain analytical assumptions must be made and processes must be embedded in their context. Context and actions interact with each other. Holistic rather than linear explanations are preferred (Pettigrew, 1997).

The Process School emphasizes strategic *thinking* over strategic *planning*. Strategic planning focuses on analysis of information, while strategic thinking focuses on synthesis. Intuition, creativity and learning are all involved. This kind of thinking requires a different understanding of hierarchies and information flows. Strategic processes are no longer exclusively top-down: successful strategies can appear at any time and at any place within the company. Thus, staff at different hierarchical levels who are involved with specific issues must be entitled to implement strategy (Mintzberg, 1994).

While former approaches to strategic management had concentrated on industry-level phenomena, strategic management in the process era was more concerned with firm-level structures. The focus moved back to examining how companies' internal mechanisms and characteristics influenced their strategy and performance. Mental models played an important role here. Members of the Process School thought that corporate-level strategic decisions emerged from complex interactions between individuals with different interests and perceptions.

Interestingly, organization theory and strategic management began to overlap. Ideas from sociology found their way into strategic planning. Companies were seen as complex, adaptive systems. This approach was reinforced by systems theory. Some basic ideas were also taken from the theory of evolution and from engineering. The New St. Gallen Management Model is a good example. The model assumes that management primarily means mastering complexity. It is based accordingly on testing systems, cybernetic discoveries and concepts. It describes organizational systems along six dimensions: environmental spheres, structuring forces, stakeholders, processes, interaction issues and modes of development (Rüegg-Sturm, 2005).

The New St. Gallen Management Model views the organization as a whole. It thus serves as an effective framework for structuring organizational communication. However, it is perhaps excessively descriptive. Systemic approaches such as the New St. Gallen Management Model are seldom used in practice by companies. This may be because they provide complicated answers to complex questions, on which basis managers find it hard to derive concrete strategic options and recommendations.

Although the approaches of the strategic process era fit better to solve the challenges of companies in an uncertain world than the approaches of traditional strategic planning did, they also have their shortcomings to do so. One of the most important shortcomings is the concentration on firm-level structures. As in today's fast-changing and globalized business world the macroeconomic, political, social

FIGURE 2.2: THE NEW ST. GALLEN MANAGEMENT MODEL

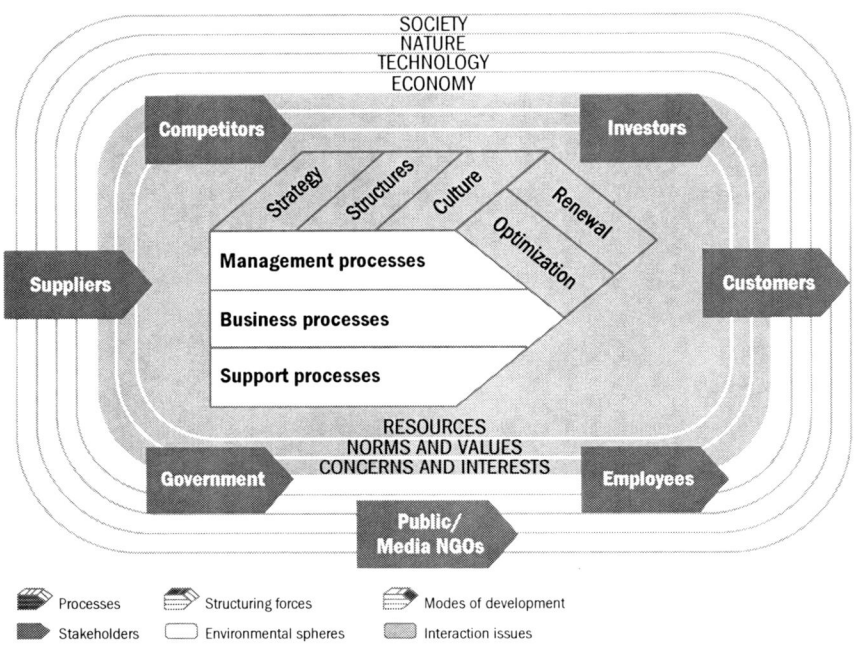

Source: Rüegg-Sturm, 2005

and natural environment is too important to be neglected. Systemic approaches like the New St. Gallen Model incorporate the environmental sphere, but these models are often too complex to be used in practice.

2.2.3
THE MULTI-PERSPECTIVE VIEW

As we have seen, research into the strategy process has added a human element into the equation. However, not enough was still understood about the unique characteristics of managerial activity. Analysts have questioned the practical relevance and usability of strategic planning. Pascale, for example, shows that it was precisely the absence of strategic planning that led to successful strategy creation at Honda (Pascale, 1984). Similarly, Hamel and Prahalad observe that large companies in the 1990s started to downsize their strategic planning departments (Hamel/Prahalad, 1994). In much the same vein, Murray speaks of "the end of management." He expects the traditional bureaucratic structures to be replaced by something more like ad hoc teams of peers who come together to tackle individual projects, and then disband (Murray, 2010).

These criticisms of strategic planning have led to a decline in research in this area (Whittington and Cailluet, 2008). The field is increasingly fragmented. Competing theoretical frameworks exist and it has become difficult to apply the approach across the whole strategy process. Instead, tools have been developed for specific purposes. The trade-off of specialization was a loss of the picture of the organization and its strategy as a whole. Some examples might make this clearer:

- **Strategy maps:** Strategy maps are an improved version of the Balanced Scorecard (BSC). They were developed by Richard Norton and David Kaplan in 1992. The idea is that companies need tools for communicating their strategy and the processes and systems that will help them implement that strategy. Strategy maps combine the traditional dimensions of the BSC (learning and growth perspective, internal process perspective, customer perspective, financial perspective) with the strategic goals of companies. They also take intangible assets into account. Strategy maps provide a visual representation of a company's key objectives and the crucial relationships between them that drive organizational performance (Kaplan/Norton, 2000). Their disadvantages are that they are strongly formalized and don't leave enough room for dynamic processes.
- **Blue Ocean Strategy:** Blue Ocean Strategy takes a close look at a company's competitive environment. It focuses on identifying untapped innovative business models ("blue oceans") by providing a wide range of tools. The goal is to find new fields where there is no competition as yet. The central paradigm is that the ideas and actions of individual players can shape the economic and industrial landscape. Executives then need to make sure that their organizations are aligned behind this strategic approach in order to produce a sustainable performance (Kim/Mauborgne, 2009). The downside of Blue Ocean Strategy is that it focuses on developing breakthrough opportunities and neglects to embed them in the standard business of the organization.

- **Business wargaming:** Wargaming focuses on the players within the competitive game. It uses role-play to simulate a situation. The approach was initially developed for use in military contexts. Business wargames are most often conducted at one of two points in an organization's planning process: at its outset and after a basic plan has been drawn up. A number of teams are created, each with up to 20 executives and senior managers. Each team is assigned the identity of a specific player, usually one of the company's competitors. The teams engage in a series of strategic moves and countermoves, navigating their way through complex strategy landscapes. The idea is that the teams in this way predict the reactions of competitors to changing market conditions. The teams move along a simulated multiyear trajectory: strategic horizons of more than 20 years are not uncommon. Wargaming does not produce a concrete business strategy. Instead, it focuses on the behavior of competitors. It gives participants a deeper understanding of the competitive dynamics behind strategy development. They can then use these insights to fashion robust strategies. But as wargaming emphasizes on human factor it neglects macroeconomic and industry level criteria.

Looking at the strengths and weaknesses of the three tools we described above we can see that they are not able to lead companies through an uncertain environment. Either they don't consider dynamic processes or they only deal with specialized fields of business.

2.3
TECHNIQUES OF PREDICTING THE FUTURE

After having seen that the approaches and tools of strategic planning have crucial limitations to cope with the uncertainty and dynamic of a company's environment we will now check whether techniques of predicting the future fulfill the needs of companies.

Companies need to reduce uncertainty so that they do not underestimate (or overestimate) the impact of changes. Different techniques have been brought up and are used for predicting the future. Below, we look at four selected methods: extrapolation, prediction markets, futurology and simulation.

- **Extrapolation** is an effective technique for predicting the future as long as the environment is stable. It involves using past experience to estimate future data. Strict underlying assumptions are needed. For example, forecasters foresee a lack of skilled workers in Germany; this forecast is based on the assumption that parameters such as migration, education and the birth rates will not change substantially in the future. Thus, the quality of the extrapolation is limited by the assumptions on which it is based.
- **Prediction markets** (or **virtual markets**) are speculative marketplaces where participants trade in contracts whose outcome depends on unknown future events. They are based on the efficient-market hypothesis: In a truly efficient prediction market, the market price will be the best predictor of the event and no combination of available polls or other information will improve on the market-generated forecasts. Prediction markets use the "wisdom of crowds" (Surowiecki, 2004) and often turn out to be more accurate than surveys.
- **Futurology** is a method developed by historians. It looks at possible, probable and preferable futures (the 3 Ps). Futurologists examine quantitative and qualitative data about the possibility, probability and desirability of change. In this way, they try to achieve a holistic view of possible futures. Wildcards (W) are used to model unpredictable factors that influence future developments: events with low probability but a high impact.
- **Simulations** are simplified approximations of a real thing, state of affairs or process. They can reveal the effects of different conditions and courses of action. Companies can use the large quantities of data they hold on customer loyalty, employee retention and supply chain management to carry out simulations and so make meaningful predictions about the behavior of any given customer or employee, or determine the likelihood of gaps in service or supply. Simulations can reveal patterns in pricing, buying habits, geographic region, household income, and so on. The assumptions are usually transformed into algorithms and the simulation is carried out by computer.

Each of the techniques above is good for working on specific problems in situations where clear assumptions are possible. However, strategic decisions of a company being in an uncertain environment require a more sophisticated and broader approach.

2.4 CONCLUSIONS

As we have seen, the first decade of the twenty-first century has been characterized by uncertainty in many different shapes: rapid globalization, accelerating innovation and growing competition, bringing with them volatility, complexity and ambiguity. Neither the aforementioned tools of strategic planning, nor the techniques of predicting the future provide an adequate solution for strategic planning in this uncertain environment. A company using these tools to plan strategy in the year 2000 could not have foreseen the eurozone crisis, dot-com bubble, exponential growth in IT, the emergence of biotechnology and nanotechnology, new business models such as eBay, Dell and Amazon, and the most dramatic global economic slump since the Great Depression. If the old systems had worked, companies would have realized that venerable institutions such as Lehman Brothers and Bear Stearns could disappear overnight. They would have foreseen that new players such as Facebook and Twitter could come out of nowhere and become giant players within less than ten years (Murray, 2010).

Companies therefore need another approach to cope with the uncertain future: scenario-based strategic planning. Scenario-based strategic planning enables companies to develop different pictures of the future and to prepare their organizations for the different futures. The approach has great potential to increase the quality of decisions and companies' performance. As we will see in the next chapter scenario-based planning overcomes the shortcomings of the aforementioned strategic planning approaches and prediction techniques. We will introduce a modern scenario-based strategic planning approach which incorporates the strengths of traditional scenario techniques and combines them with new elements in a holistic approach to make it a powerful tool for today's strategic planning.

2.5 REFERENCES

Acemoglu D., Ozdaglar A., Tahbaz-Salehi A. 2010. Cascade in networks and aggregate volatility. *NBER Working Paper* No. 16516.

Ambrosini V., Billsberry J. 2008. *Value congruence and its impact on causal ambiguity*. Paper on 2nd Global e-Conference on Fit. http://www.fitsconference.com/2008/fri01.pdf. Accessed 20 July 2011.

Andrews KR. 1971. *The concept of corporate strategy*. Homewood: Dow Jones-Irwin.

Comin D., Philippon T. 2006. The rise in firm-level volatility: causes and consequences. *NBER Macroeconomics Annual 2005*. Vol. 20. http://www.nber.org/books/gert06-1. Accessed 20 July 2011.

Courtney H., Kirkland J., Viguerie P. 1997. Strategy under uncertainty. *Harvard Business Review* 75(6): 66-79.

Cummings S., Daellenbach U. 2009. A guide to the future of strategy? The history of Long Range Planning. *Long Range Planning* 42(2): 234-263.

Gartner Group. 2010. *Gartner top end user predictions for 2010: coping with the new balance of power*. http://www.gartner.com/it/page.jsp?id=1278413. Accessed 20 July 2011.

Gausemeier J. 2010. Undenkbares denken. *Harvard Business Manager*, 32(10): 28-32.

Ghemawat P. 2011. *World 3.0 – Global prosperity and how to achieve it*. Boston: Harvard Business School Press.

Hamel G., Prahalad CK. 1994. *Competing for the future*. Boston: Harvard Business School Press.

Hemp P. 2009. Death by information overload. *Harvard Business Review* 87(9): 82-89.

Incorrect predictions. 2013. *Wikiquote*. http://www.billionquotes.com/index.php/Incorrect_predictions. Accessed 15 March 2013.

International Energy Agency (IEA). 2012. *World Energy Outlook 2012*. Paris: IEA.

International Telecommunication Union (ITU). 2012. *Measuring the Information Society 2012*. Geneva: ITU.

Jacobides MG. 2010. Strategy tools for a shifting landscape. *Harvard Business Review* 88(1): 76-84.

Lippmann SA., Rumelt RP. 1982. Uncertain imitability. An analysis of interfirm differences in efficiency under competition. *Bell Journal of Economics* 13(2): 418-438.

Kaplan RS., Norton DP. 1993. Putting the balanced scorecard to work. *Harvard Business Review* 71(9): 134-147.

Kim WC., Mauborgne R. 2009. How strategy shapes structure. *Harvard Business Review* 87(9): 72–80.

Marx K., Engels F. 1969. *Selected Works Vol. 1.* Moscow: Progress Publishers.

Milliken FJ. 1987. Three types of perceived uncertainty about the environment: state, effect, and response uncertainty. *The Academy of Management Review* 12(1): 133-143.

Mintzberg H. 1994. The fall and the rise of strategic planning. *Harvard Business Review* 72(1): 107-114.

Murray A. 2010. The end of management. *Wall Street Journal online* http://online.wsj.com/article/SB10001424052748704476104575439723695579664.html. Accessed 20 July 2011.

Newman R. 2011. Why US companies aren't so American anymore. *Money, US News and World Report.* http://money.usnews.com/money/blogs/flowchart/2011/06/30/why-us-companies-arent-so-american-anymore. Accessed 23 November 2012.

Pascale RT. 1984. Perspective on strategy: the real story behind Honda's success. *California Management Review* 26(3): 47-72.

Pettigrew A. 1997. What is a processual analysis? *Scandinavian Journal of Management* 13(4): 337–48.

Porter M. 2008. The five competitive forces that shape strategy. *Harvard Business Review* 86(1): 79-93.

Ribgy D., Bilodeau B. 2007. Selecting management tools wisely, *Harvard Business Review* 85(12): 20-22.

Roland Berger Strategy Consultants. 2011. *Trend Compendium 2030.* http://www.rolandberger.com/expertise/functional_issues/trend_compendium_2030/index.html. Accessed 20 July 2011.

Rüegg-Sturm J. 2005. *The new St. Gallen management model: basic categories of an approach to integrated management.* Basingstoke: Palgrave Macmillan.

Schrader S., Riggs WM., Smith RP. 1993. Choice over uncertainty and ambiguity in technical problem solving. *Journal of Engineering and Technology Management* 10(2): 73-99.

Snowden DJ., Boone ME. 2007. A leader's framework for decision making. *Harvard Business Review* 85(11), 68-76.

Surowiecki J. 2004. *The wisdom of crowds*. New York: Doubleday.

Whittington R., Cailluet L. 2008. The crafts of strategy. *Long Range Planning* 41(3): 241-247.

Wüst C. 2006. Germany's new Mercedes museum: From horsepower to Pope mobil. *Spiegel Online International.* http://www.spiegel.de/international/spiegel/germany-s-new-mercedes-museum-from-horsepower-to-the-popemobile-a-416896.html. Accessed 15 March 2013.

3. Scenario-based strategic planning: A new approach to coping with uncertainty

TORSTEN WULF, PHILIP MEISSNER,
CHRISTIAN BRANDS AND STEPHAN STUBNER

In today's increasingly dynamic, volatile and complex business world, companies in many industries face new challenges when it comes to strategic planning. Scenario planning is a popular approach used by companies to meet these challenges. However, traditional approaches to scenario planning are complex and focus on the long term. Our solution is an enhanced, scenario-based strategic planning approach that integrates scenario planning into strategic planning. The approach is tool-based and therefore easy for firms to apply. We illustrate our approach with examples from different industries.

3.1 INTRODUCTION

In this chapter we present an approach to scenario-based strategic planning that integrates scenario planning into strategic planning. This new approach provides a framework that enables managers to deal more effectively with the challenges posed by an increasingly uncertain business environment, characterized by complexity and volatility.

Strategic planning is one of the most influential and widely used tools of management (Rigby/Bilodeau, 2007). The 1970s and '80s saw the development of popular frameworks such as Porter's Five Forces and the SWOT analysis (Porter, 1979; Porter, 1980). Their objective was to identify the best single strategy for a company (Porter, 1980). Today's corporate managers operate in an increasingly volatile, uncertain and complex environment (Chermack, 2011). Researchers argue that, in such conditions, traditional approaches to strategic planning are unable to produce high-quality strategic decisions. Specifically, they criticize the belief, underlying traditional strategic planning approaches, that plans should be developed for a single future direction (Camillus/Datta, 1991; Eisenhardt/Sull, 2001; Grant, 2003).

Today's companies need new instruments for strategic planning, instruments that will allow them to plan in an environment of uncertainty. They can no longer forecast developments on the basis of single projections: they must consider multiple plausible futures. Different strategic options increase flexibility of implementation. Planning needs to become more comprehensive (Elbanna/Child, 2007; Miller, 2008) and quicker (Shimizu/Hitt, 2004; Ghobadian et al., 2008; Dye et al., 2009), so that companies can adapt rapidly to changing environmental conditions.

Scenario planning is an important part of strategic planning today (Schoemaker, 1995; Cornelius et al., 2005). It provides a sound basis for comprehensive planning. By analyzing multiple future developments and fostering a strategic discussion, it gives firms a holistic understanding of potential future changes (Wack, 1985; van der Heijden, 2005).

Traditional scenario planning approaches have a number of weaknesses, however. For example, they can be highly complex and slow (Millet, 2003; Verity, 2003; Bradfield, 2008). Scenario projects usually last a minimum of five months, and sometimes as long as a year (Moyer, 1996). Therefore, traditional scenario planning needs to be adapted if it is to be integrated effectively into modern strategic planning.

A modified approach to scenario planning has the potential to significantly improve strategy building within companies. Such an approach should be standardized and tool-based. Our scenario-based approach to strategic planning meets these requirements. It enables companies to formulate a core strategy, complemented by a number of strategic options derived from different strategic scenarios. This framework is highly beneficial for strategic planning (Birkinshaw et al., 2008; Whittington/Cailluet, 2008).

Below, we take a closer look at traditional forms of scenario planning. We identify similarities between the different approaches and pinpoint any shortcomings. We then present our new approach to scenario-based strategic planning. We show how firms can apply the approach within a standard strategic planning process. Process steps are illustrated with examples from the German electronic retail and long-distance heating industry. The examples show how our new approach enables companies to react flexibly to changes taking place around them and achieve lasting competitive advantage.

3.2 SCENARIO PLANNING – THE BASIS FOR MODERN STRATEGIC PLANNING

Scenario planning was first introduced by Royal Dutch Shell in the 1970s to complement traditional forecasting tools. With the help of this approach, the company was able to react earlier and more effectively to the 1973 oil crisis than its competitors (Wack, 1985a).

Scenario planning is a method for developing and analyzing possible future states and development paths (Schoemaker, 1995). Its aim is not to accurately predict the future, but rather to better understand the logical paths that lead to different scenarios and to help develop more comprehensive strategies (Porter, 1985; Wack, 1985a; Schoemaker, 1995).

Unlike traditional strategic planning methods, scenario planning develops different possible views of the future, thus providing a basis for generating strategies that deal with different contingencies (van der Heijden, 2005). It takes uncertainty into account and allows strategists to deal more effectively with complexity, volatility and change when making strategic choices (Porter, 1985). In turn, this leads to increased responsiveness and alertness to changes in market conditions (Grant, 2003).

Furthermore, scenario planning takes the different perspectives of internal and external stakeholders into account. Thus, it can foster cognitive change in the "mental models" of decision makers – it challenges their assumptions and broadens their perception of possible developments (Wack, 1985a; Schoemaker, 1993; Ringland, 1998).

The last 40 years have seen a number of different approaches to scenario planning (Bishop et al., 2007). Among the most influential have been those of Royal Dutch Shell (Shell International, 2003) and the consulting firm Global Business Network (Schwartz, 1996). Millet (2003) calls these two approaches the "gold standard of corporate scenario generation." Two academic approaches are also particularly important, those of van der Heijden and Schoemaker (Chermack et al., 2001).

Although they differ in terms of detail, the various approaches to scenario planning share some common features. Thus, they all consist of a number of process steps, of which six can be identified in total, although no one approach contains all six steps (Phelps et al., 2001; Chermack et al., 2001; Millet, 2003; Bishop et al., 2007). The six steps are as follows:

Definition of scope: The first step is to define the scope of the scenario project. This phase is known in some approaches as "preparation" (Shell International, 2003). It creates the foundation for the analysis and strategy definition phases by specifying key elements in the project such as the timeframe, scope and team involved (Schoemaker, 1995; Schwartz, 1996; Shell International, 2003; van der Heijden, 2005).

Perception analysis: This phase is also known as "pioneering" (Shell International, 2003) or "identifying the major stakeholders" (Schoemaker, 1995). Its purpose is to analyze the perceptions of the managers involved in the scenario project. Their "mental models" are identified and then challenged by confronting them with other models, such as those derived from external opinions. In this way, the managers learn about the interests and expectations of external stakeholders and gain insights into their own assumptions. This gives them a more holistic view of possible maps of the future (Schoemaker, 1995; Shell International, 2003).

Trend and uncertainty analysis: This step is found in all major approaches to scenario planning. Sometimes it consists of two parts, as in Schoemaker's "identify basic trends" and "identify key uncertainties" (Schoemaker, 1995). Alternatively it consists of a single step, as in van der Heijden's "data analysis" (van der Heijden, 2005). The scenario team analyzes the key drivers affecting the company or industry. These factors are then ranked by degree of uncertainty and potential impact on the company. Thus, the key drivers are identified that must be considered in the company's planning (Schoemaker, 1995; Schwartz, 1996; Shell International, 2003; van der Heijden, 2005).

Scenario building: This forms the core step of traditional approaches to scenario planning. The uncertainties identified in the preceding step are converted into distinct scenarios that describe different future states of the world. Other driving forces are added so as to create consistent, plausible stories about the future. Potential developments are also considered, linking the present to a specific picture of the future (Schwartz, 1996; Shell International, 2003). The "scenario building" step broadens the participants' perceptions and creates the foundation for the subsequent "strategy definition" phase, in which possible consequences and action plans for each scenario are developed (Schoemaker, 1995; Shell International, 2003).

Strategy definition: This step is also known as "implications" (Schwartz, 1996) or "option planning" (van der Heijden, 2005). Companies test possible decisions or strategic options against the various scenarios that have been generated. This makes the company's strategy more robust and means that it can be applied in various potential future situations (Schwartz, 1996). It also means that the people responsible for strategy in the company can act more flexibly and have recourse to different strategic options depending on what happens in the future.

Monitoring: Some approaches include this sixth step. It is also known as "selection of leading indicators and signposts" (e.g. at GBN; Schwartz, 1996) or "reconnaissance" (e.g. at Royal Dutch Shell; Shell International, 2003). The company defines a number of indicators and then monitors them to check whether strategic changes are needed. Schoemaker (1995) and van der Heijden (2005) draw attention to the importance of monitoring the environment continuously and repeating the scenario process if drastic changes occur.

Scenario planning offers a number of benefits. However, as discussed further above, they can be complex and require a substantial investment in terms of time and resources, generally lasting between five months and a year (Bradfield, 2008; Moyer, 1996; Shell International, 2003). A major reason for this complexity appears to be the lack of standardization in most scenario planning approaches. Many analysts draw attention to the fact that there are no set recipes for creating scenarios (Schwartz, 1996). Very few scenario planning approaches offer standardized tools, and where they do, these tools are only relevant for specific process steps (Schoemaker, 1995;

van der Heijden, 2005). Many scenario experts are also unwilling to disclose the full methodology they use (Chermack et al., 2001). This makes traditional scenario planning techniques hard to replicate. Consequently, scenario processes vary widely and their quality depends greatly on who precisely is involved (Schwartz, 1996).

Another drawback of scenario planning is that its timeframe typically differs from that of strategic planning. Strategic planning commonly looks at the medium-term horizon, from three to five years. Traditional scenario planning, by contrast, is almost exclusively used for long-term planning, looking at periods of five years or more (Wack, 1985a; Moyer, 1996; Schwartz, 1996).

To overcome these drawbacks, certain adaptations to traditional scenario planning approaches are required. Scenario planning must be integrated into the strategic planning process. The scenario planning approach must be built on a systematic process. Clear frameworks must be defined for the individual process steps, reducing the complexity and time needed for implementation. We call this adapted approach "scenario-based strategic planning" and discuss it in detail in the following section.

3.3 DESIGNING A SCENARIO-BASED APPROACH TO STRATEGIC PLANNING

3.3.1 OVERVIEW

In this section we present a scenario-based approach to strategic planning. This approach consists of a structured process with standardized frameworks for its application. It enables corporate strategists to directly integrate scenario planning into the strategic planning process and thus meet the requirements of complex and volatile environments.

The scenario-based approach to strategic planning builds on the advantages of traditional scenario planning. By creating different scenarios, it allows decision makers to plan for multiple contingencies. At the same time, however, it broadens the perceptions of strategists by integrating the perspectives of internal and external stakeholders into the planning process. In this way it creates a more "open" form of strategic planning.

Our approach is based on the six steps found in traditional scenario planning, as described above. For each of the six process steps we apply specific frameworks. Two of these frameworks are taken from traditional scenario planning. They are complemented by four new frameworks developed by us. The frameworks provide the structure for the analysis carried out in each step. They enhance and simplify the process of generating scenarios. This makes the process easier and quicker to apply in practice. Figure 3.1 gives an overview of the six steps and the related frameworks.

In our experience, the time required to carry out the scenario planning process using our new approach is just four to six weeks, roughly the same amount of time as is typically needed for the strategic planning process (Grant, 2003; Ocasio/ Joseph, 2008). Our approach also meets the challenges of increasing volatility, rapid change and complexity of the environment. It does this by integrating different stakeholders into the planning process and allowing for different outcomes. This results in a comprehensive set of strategic options rather than a single option.

Below, we present each of the six steps and related frameworks in turn. For the purposes of illustration, we look at two actual case studies based on projects that we have carried out ourselves. The industries involved are characterized by a high degree of volatility, rapid change and complex environments: the German long-distance heating and the German electronic retail sector.

STEP 1: DEFINITION OF SCOPE

In Step 1 we define the overall scope of the project. Our framework is the *framing checklist*. This checklist ensures that all key aspects are covered. It specifies the goal, strategic level of analysis, participants, time horizon and stakeholders to be included in the process. It consists of five questions (see Figure 3.2). The strategic planning team must answer these questions and receive approval from the top management team before the actual planning process begins.

FIGURE 3.1: THE HHL-ROLAND BERGER SCENARIO-DEVELOPMENT PROCESS

Task: Identify core problems and frame analysis
Result: Clear project goal
Framework: Framing checklist

Task: Identify assumptions and mental models
Result: Holistic understanding of internal and external perspectives; blind spots and weak signals identified
Framework: 360° stakeholder feedback

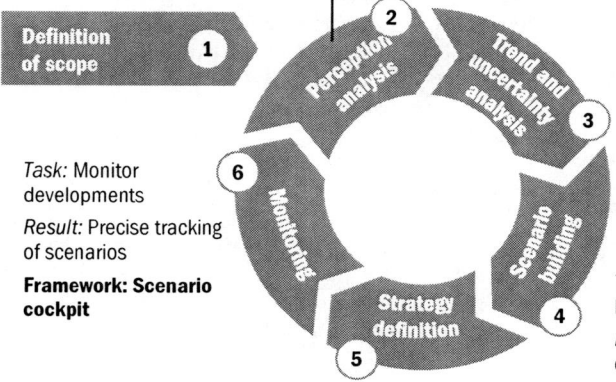

Task: Discuss and evaluate relevant trends
Result: Key trends and critical uncertainties identified and analyzed
Framework: Impact/uncertainly grid

Task: Monitor developments
Result: Precise tracking of scenarios
Framework: Scenario cockpit

Task: Develop scenarios based on key uncertainties
Result: Detailed description of four scenarios
Framework: Scenario matrix

Task: Derive action plans for implementation
Result: Comprehensive strategy alternatives for different contingencies
Framework: Strategy manual

Defining the project goal is particularly important as it sets the scope for the entire analysis. This may be global or focused on specific regions, countries or such like. For example, in our project in the consumer electronics retail industry, the scope was limited to stationary consumer electronics retailers in Germany and existing online operations were excluded from the planning process.

The framework ensures that all participants in the process – typically corporate and business unit managers as well as strategic planners – are "on the same page" as far as the goals of the strategic planning process are concerned. To ensure relevance for strategic planning, we usually set the time horizon at three to five years. However, for industries with shorter planning cycles, such as telecommunications or IT, this time horizon can be reduced. In terms of the strategic level of

FIGURE 3.2: FRAMING CHECKLIST

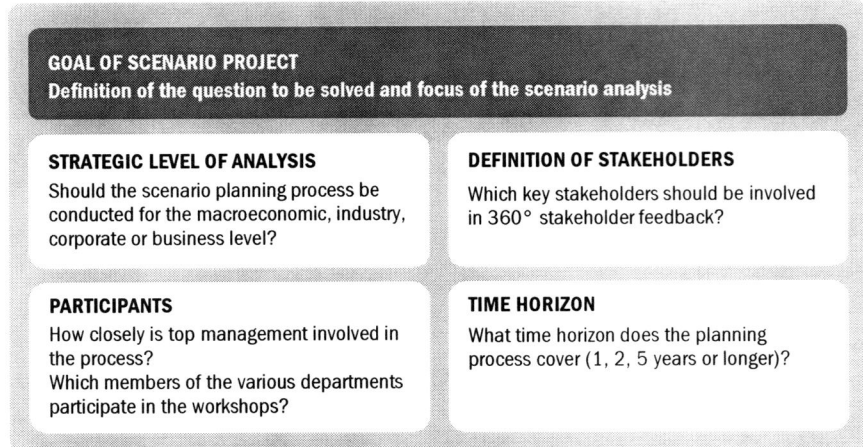

analysis, most scenario-based strategic planning is at the level of the business unit or the corporate level.

Perhaps the most important aspect of the framing checklist is defining the relevant internal and external stakeholders. The selection of stakeholders should be as broad as possible. We identify eight different categories of internal and external stakeholders: the company's management, shareholders and employees in key operating positions (e.g. marketing, sales, R&D) are internal stakeholders; its suppliers, customers, financial analysts, governmental institutions and the general public are external shareholders. In Step 2 of the process, the company contacts key individuals in these groups to gain their input.

STEP 2: PERCEPTION ANALYSIS

The goal of Step 2 is to examine the perspectives of internal and external stakeholders on future developments in the industry. This opens up the strategic planning process. The assumptions and "mental models" of internal stakeholders, particularly the top management team, are challenged by confronting them with the views of external stakeholders.

Step 2 results in a comprehensive list of factors potentially influencing the future of the industry. These factors are then evaluated in terms of their potential impact on the company's performance and their degree of uncertainty. The views of the different stakeholder groups are compared. This allows the company to identify any blind spots (areas consciously or unconsciously ignored) and weak signals (initial indicators of future changes in the environment). These factors are particularly important as they open up managers' thinking about the future and make the planning process more comprehensive.

Our framework for Step 2 is what we call *360° stakeholder feedback*. At its core lies a two-part survey, available both online and offline, that analyzes the perceptions of the internal and external stakeholders identified in the framing checklist (see Figure 3.3). First, the company sends stakeholders a questionnaire consisting of open questions about factors shaping the industry now and in the future. This questionnaire covers six micro-environmental dimensions: political, economic, social, technological, ecological and legal dimensions (PESTEL analysis). These dimensions shape the company's future but are usually beyond their control; the company simply has to adapt to them. The factors indicated by respondents as relevant are then clustered to give a total of 40 different factors. Looking at this number of factors has proven to be effective; it allows for a wide range of different factors to be considered without creating too much complexity.

Next, survey participants are sent a new questionnaire consisting of closed questions about the 40 factors. They are asked to rate each factor with regard to its impact on the company's performance and its level of uncertainty on a scale from one to ten, where one represents "low/weak" and ten "high/strong".

The 360° stakeholder feedback tool results in a list of key factors influencing the industry. With this list, the company can easily identify possible changes in the macro environment as well as any blind spots or weak signals.

In our project in the German electronic retail industry, the framework resulted in a list of factors ranging from economic factors (e.g. "market concentration on the retailers' side") to technological factors ("digitalization of new products"). We were

FIGURE 3.3: THE 360° STAKEHOLDER FEEDBACK PROCESS

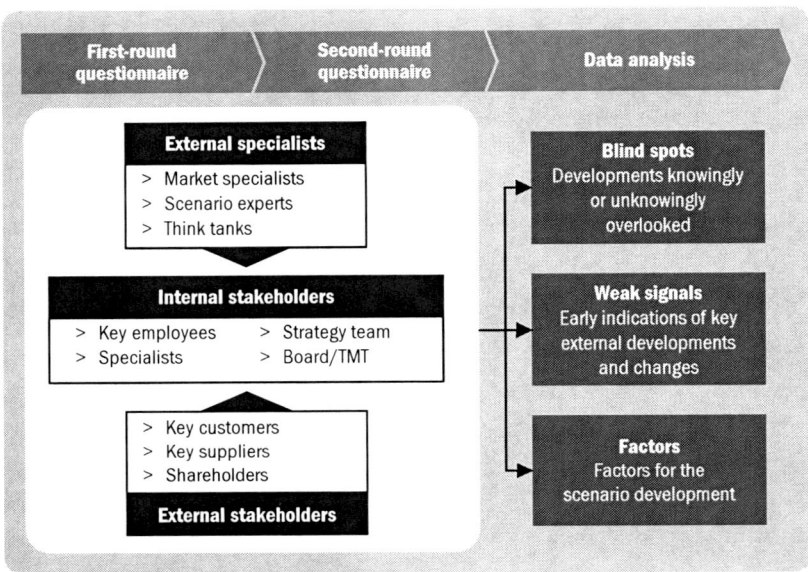

also able to identify factors rated significantly higher by external stakeholders than by the company's management, i.e. the company's blind spots. These related mainly to technological factors such as "acceptance and penetration of the mobile Internet" and "using the Internet for price comparison" (see Figure 3.4). The latter factor was also identified as a weak signal – a factor that only a few participants named in the first round of the questionnaire but which was rated highly in terms of uncertainty and impact by all participants in the second round. As a consequence, the Internet and mobile price comparison were explicitly included in Step 3 of the process. These factors subsequently formed a major part of the strategy of one major German electronic retail company that participated in our analysis.

Step 2 focuses the management's attention on key emerging trends in the industry and makes them re-examine their perceptions of how technological

FIGURE 3.4: BLIND SPOT ANALYSIS FOR THE ELECTRONICS RETAIL INDUSTRY

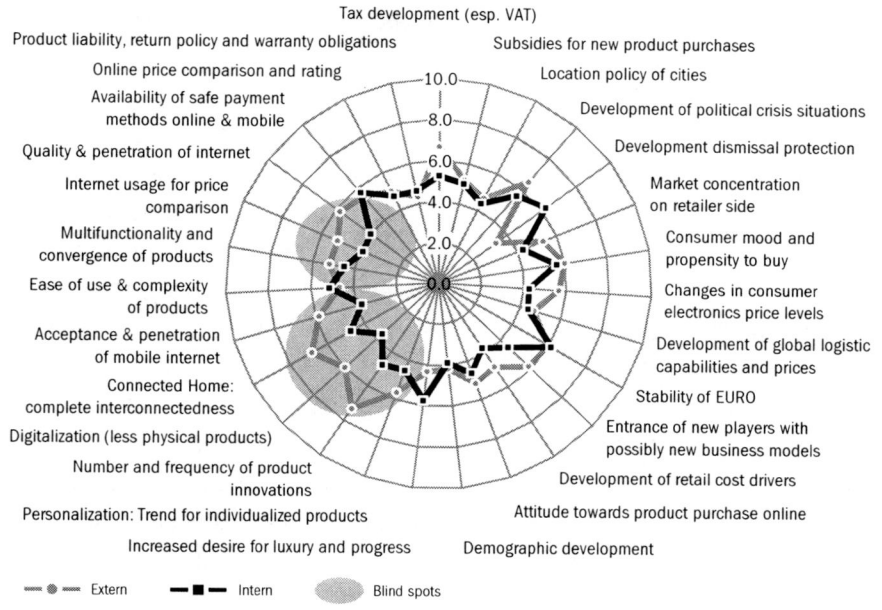

developments may impact the industry. This process promotes strategic discussion within the strategic planning and top management teams.

STEP 3: TREND AND UNCERTAINTY ANALYSIS

Step 3 structures and prioritizes the factors identified in Step 2 as a basis for determining two scenario dimensions. These two dimensions are key for creating the scenarios in Step 4.

Our framework for Step 3 is the *impact/uncertainty grid*. This was first proposed in the 1970s by Kees van der Heijden as a way of structuring the large number of input variables normally used in scenario planning. It was first applied in scenario development at Royal Dutch Shell (van 't Klooster/van Asselt, 2006). The impact/uncertainty grid systematically positions influence factors according to their impact on the company's performance and their degree of uncertainty (see Figure 3.5). The position of individual factors in the matrix is determined by their average evaluation by the stakeholders in Step 2 (the perception analysis). However, some factors will be evaluated differently by different stakeholder groups, so the members of the planning and top management teams should also discuss these automatically generated positions, revising them where necessary.

The impact/uncertainty grid is divided into three sections. The bottom section contains factors that have a relatively minor impact on the performance of the company; these "secondary elements" are not further considered in the scenario planning process. In our project in the German long-distance heating industry, for instance, secondary elements included "regional commercialization of long-distance heating products" and "reduction of transport waste in long-distance heating networks."

The upper left-hand section of the grid contains factors that have a relatively major impact on the performance of the company and which are relatively easy to predict. These are simply known as "trends". Important trends in the case of the long-distance heating industry included "under-utilization of the long-distance heating network" and "development of direct industry subsidies" These trends are later used in Step 4 in the detailed descriptions of scenarios (Schwartz, 1996).

The upper right-hand section of the grid contains the most important factors for scenario development: "critical uncertainties". These are factors with a major impact on the company and a high degree of uncertainty. They serve as the basis for identifying the two scenario dimensions, typically the result of combining or clustering closely related critical uncertainties.

In practice, we usually find between three and seven critical uncertainties per industry or business. In the long-distance heating industry, for example, we identified two political uncertainties, including the "regulation on price-fixing for long-distance heating products" and "a positive regulation for electricity generated by combined heat and power", which we then combined into the first scenario

FIGURE 3.5: IMPACT/UNCERTAINTY GRID FOR THE GERMAN LONG-DISTANCE HEATING INDUSTRY

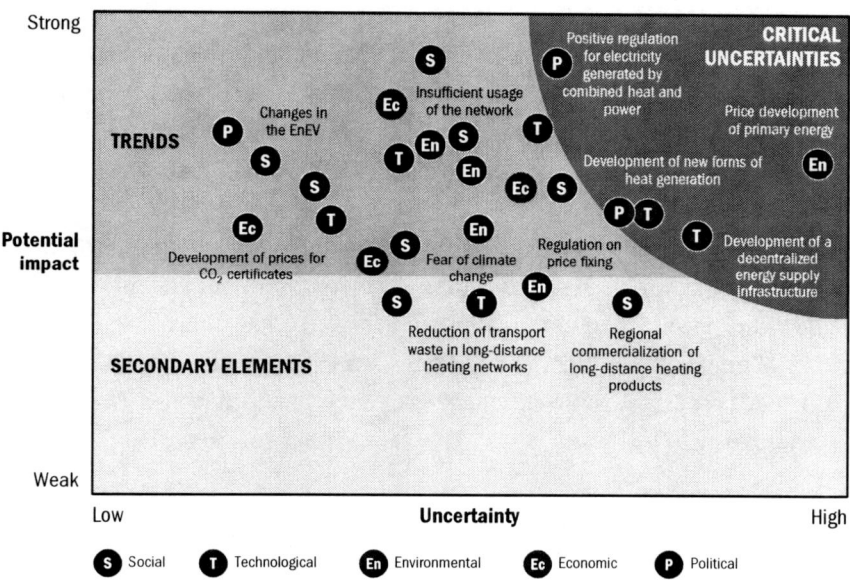

dimension: "relative price for long-distance heating products compared to other heat generation methods". We further identified three technological uncertainties, including "development of new forms of heat generation", which we combined into the second scenario dimension: "degree of autonomous heat generation."

STEP 4: SCENARIO BUILDING

In Step 4, specific scenarios are developed for the company or industry and described in detail. Our framework for this step is the *scenario matrix*. The scenario matrix uses the results of the trend and uncertainty analysis. Like the impact/uncertainty grid, the scenario matrix was developed in the 1970s by Kees van der Heijden and first used by Royal Dutch Shell (van 't Klooster/van Asselt, 2006).

SCENARIO-BASED STRATEGIC PLANNING

Two extreme values are defined for each scenario dimension; these set the boundaries for the scenario matrix. The matrix consists of four quadrants, reflecting four distinct future scenarios (van 't Klooster/van Asselt, 2006). Four is generally regarded as the maximum number of scenarios that decision makers are able to process (Wack, 1985b; van der Heijden, 2005). Each of the scenarios is assigned a distinctive name. In our project in the German long-distance heating industry, for example, we used the two scenario dimensions "relative price for long-distance heating products compared to other heat generation methods" and "degree of autonomous heat generation". We named the four resulting scenarios "Long-Distance Heat 2.0", "Ecological Renaissance", "Decline" and "Clearance Sale" (see Figure 3.6). The different sectors of the matrix ease the creation of scenarios as they visualize distinct future environments.

Using the scenario matrix, we then add detail to the scenarios. This is done in two steps. First, an "influence diagram" is created, showing the series of causes and effects that lead to different situations with regard to the dimensions. The trends and critical uncertainties identified in Step 3 are an integral part of these relationships. The main purpose of the influence diagram is to ensure consistency between the scenarios.

In our project in the German long-distance heating industry, the influence diagram included the factors "changes in sales volume" and "structural developments in the energy sector." Both of these factors have an impact on the development of the regulatory environment in Germany. Figure 3.7 gives an example of a simplified influence diagram from the German long-distance heating industry.

We then create a storyline for each scenario, based on the influence diagram. Different storylines can be created by changing how the factors in the influence diagram develop. The storylines are used to add detail to the scenarios. For example, the following are summarized descriptions of the four scenarios that we developed in 2012 for the German long-distance industry (scenarios are for the year 2021 from the perspective of German long-distance heat producers located in the former eastern part of Germany):

- *Long-Distance Heat 2.0* describes a future where long-distance heat producers can expand their market power in eastern Germany. Having stopped the emigration

FIGURE 3.6: SCENARIO MATRIX FOR THE GERMAN LONG-DISTANCE HEATING INDUSTRY IN 2021

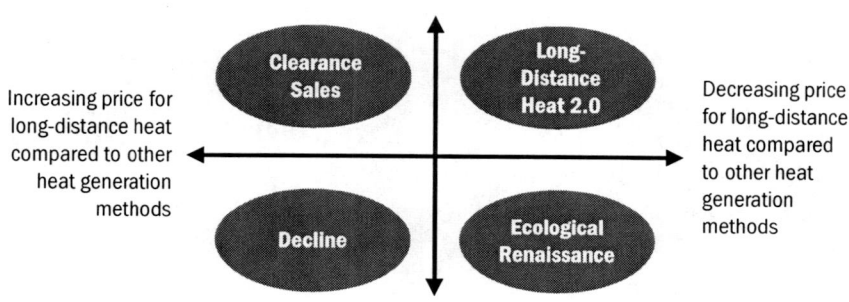

of habitants from urban areas in eastern Germany and using renewable energy sources in the process of generating long-distance heat, helps producers to attract new customers. In this scenario the German government actively supports combined heat and power generation meaning long-distance heat producers face minimal regulatory barriers.

♦ *Ecological Renaissance* describes a highly competitive market where long-distance heat producers can absorb customer losses by using renewable energy sources. However, due to high energy prices and energy black-outs as a consequence of an overloaded electricity grid customers increasingly produce their electricity and heat by themselves. Regulation is focused on creating a reliable and cost efficient energy infrastructure rather than on supporting specific power generation systems.

♦ *Decline* is a world in which German long-distance heat producers slowly disappear. Customers favor autonomous energy and heat production and no longer want to rely on energy companies. Fast technological developments in the field of decentralized energy production technology such as block heating power plants make these technologies affordable for small households. Regulation favors decentralized energy production to break the market power of the big energy companies.

FIGURE 3.7: SIMPLIFIED INFLUENCE DIAGRAM FOR THE GERMAN LONG-DISTANCE HEATING INDUSTRY

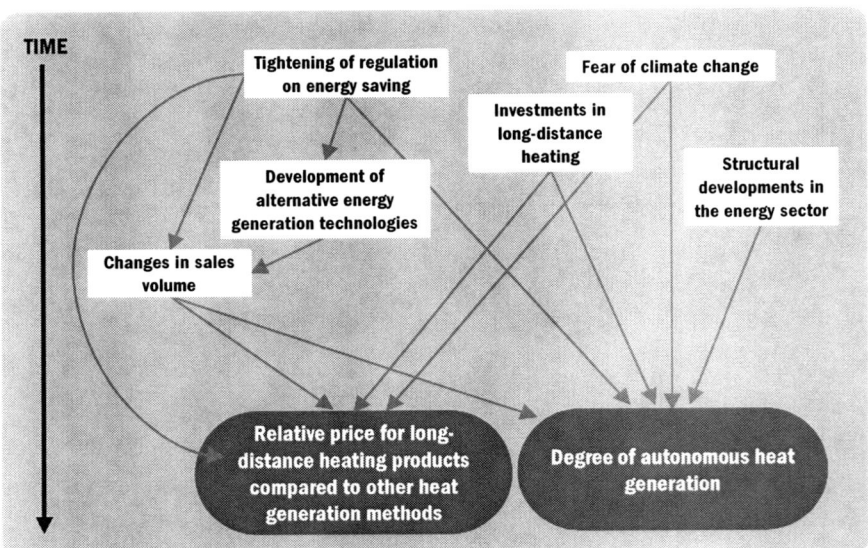

- *Clearance Sale* describes a future where German long-distance heat producers can no longer compete against conventional heating systems due to technological advancements. Germany's electricity grid could not cope with the massive use of renewable energy leading to severe black-outs. These developments led to increasing governmental support for traditional energy production technologies meaning long-distance heat becomes a niche product that slowly fades out.

STEP 5: STRATEGY DEFINITION
In Step 5, the company derives concrete strategies and options for each of the four scenarios. This step takes the company from merely thinking about the future to developing concrete action plans.

Our framework is the *strategy manual*. First, the company derives specific strategic recommendations for each of the scenarios. Next, it compares these four sets of strategic recommendations and identifies common elements. Experience shows that the shorter the planning cycle, the more strategy elements will be common to all scenarios. Finally, the company takes these common strategy elements and forms them into a core strategy. The company can implement this core strategy whatever happens, irrespective of developments in any of the scenarios.

In our project in the long-distance heating industry, we drew up a strategy manual for companies active in the industry and politicians using the method described above. First, we derived strategic recommendations for each of the four scenarios, then we compared them to identify common elements, and finally we formed a core strategy – in this case, an intelligent regulation of the industry to ensure it supports Germany's efforts towards using more renewable energy sources. Industry regulation is a core element of the future development of the industry meaning companies need to clearly communicate their goals to regulators. Moreover companies have to become more active in using renewable sources as part of their heat generation processes. Supported by an adequate public relations campaign the industry has to ensure that it is seen as an enabler of Germany's future energy policy rather than an outdated technology. This strategy was found to be robust for all four scenarios.

The strategy elements that are *not* common to all scenarios can now be taken and used to develop scenario-specific strategic options that complement the core strategy. Depending on the environment, some of these strategic options should be executed immediately. Others require a certain level of investment, and still others can be filed – with an option for implementing them later on, should they become relevant.

In the case of our project in the long-distance heating industry, the core strategy was complemented by scenario-specific strategy options. As for the long-distance heating industry, we developed an "Ecological Renaissance" scenario (see above). In this scenario, high energy prices and an inefficient electricity grid dominate. Two strategic options deliver positive results: The usage of renewable energy sources as part of the generation process of long-distance heat and the constant technological advancement of combined power and heat production facilities. Both allow industry participants to be part of Germany's effort to use more renewable resources and improve energy efficiency.

By increasing the number of strategic options available, the strategy manual enables companies to react quickly to changes taking place around them. This means that they are better able to meet the challenges posed by an increasingly dynamic, complex and volatile environment.

STEP 6: MONITORING

Step 6 is the final step. It takes the company from strategy creation to strategy implementation. The aim of this step is to monitor developments in the industry and determine whether any adjustments to strategies are needed.

Our framework for Step 6 is the *scenario cockpit*. This consists of key indicators for changes in the company's environment. It reveals which of the scenarios is closest to the developments taking place in the real world. In most cases, the company can derive these indicators directly from the influence diagram (Step 4). For each indicator in each scenario, a maximum range for the values must be set. Comparing these ranges with the actual values then reveals which scenario is closest to reality and which strategy option should be implemented alongside the core strategy.

In our project in the long-distance heating industry, indicators included changes in the electricity price on the spot market or technological advancements in competing technologies leading to higher efficiencies when producing heat or electricity. Companies operating in the long-distance heat industry can now regularly monitor the suggested indicators so they can implement the relevant strategy options quickly when necessary.

The scenario cockpit determines which strategic options need to be executed and when, depending on developments in the environment. It also helps companies assess whether the scenarios are still valid and plausible or if they should be revised.

FIGURE 3.8: THE SCENARIO-BASED STRATEGIC PLANNING PROCESS

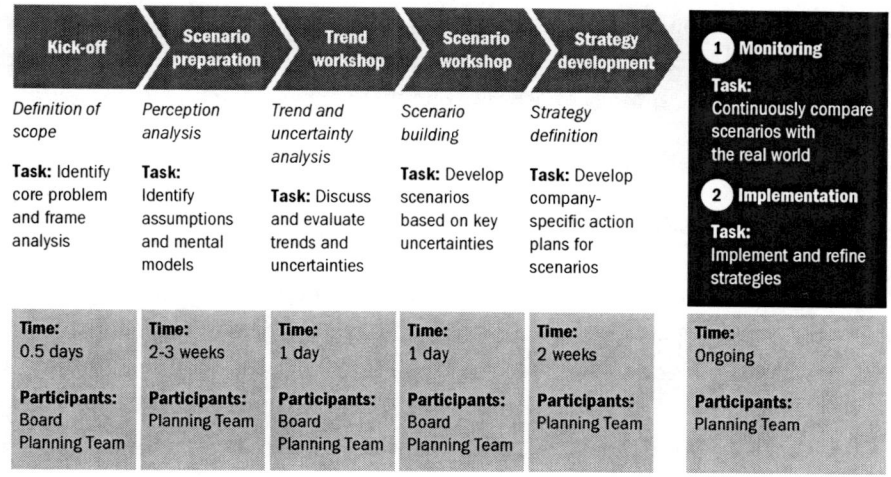

3.3.2
INTEGRATING THE APPROACH INTO THE STRATEGIC PLANNING PROCESS

Scenario-based strategic planning can be integrated into companies' planning processes in six steps. This is simple to implement and takes just four to six weeks (see Figure 3.8).

The scenario-based strategic planning process is carried out by a planning team. This team coordinates the process and conducts the necessary analyses. The top management team and the heads of business units should attend the kick-off meeting and the two workshops – the "trend workshop" and the "scenario workshop" – where the scenario dimensions and the scenarios are drawn up. All major decisions are taken at these workshops.

To prepare for the scenario workshop, the planning team uses the 360° stakeholder feedback tool. At the workshop, the scenarios are drawn up and initial steps for strategy implementation are derived. After the workshop, the planning team defines the core strategy and corresponding strategy options. The strategy proposal is then presented to the Board, which decides which strategy and action plans to pursue. Strategy implementation goes hand-in-hand with constant monitoring of developments in the real world using the scenario cockpit. This enables the planning team to adjust the chosen strategy depending on what happens in the environment.

3.4 CONCLUSION

In this chapter we present our new, scenario-based approach to strategic planning. This approach integrates scenario planning into strategic planning. It thus rises to the challenges presented by increasingly uncertain business environments.

Our new approach avoids the problems associated with traditional scenario planning, which can be highly complex and time-consuming. It is a clearly structured and tool-based process that is easy to apply and can be integrated into a company's standard strategic planning process.

Our six-step process is rooted in traditional scenario planning frameworks. It allows companies not only to generate the best strategy, but also to plan for different potential future developments. At the same time, it integrates other perspectives into the strategic planning process. This means that the company's planning takes all eventualities into account and can react faster to changes in the environment – giving the company a distinct advantage over its competitors in an increasingly uncertain world.

3.5 REFERENCES

Bishop P., Hines A., Collins T. 2007. The Current State of Scenario Development. An Overview of Techniques. *Foresight* 9(1): 5-25.

Birkinshaw J., Hamel G., Mol MJ. 2008. Management Innovation. *Academy of Management Review* 33(4): 825-845.

Bradfield RM. 2008. Cognitive Barriers in the Scenario Development Process. *Advances in Developing Human Resources* 10(2): 198-215.

Camillus JC., Datta DK. 1991. Managing strategic issues in a turbulent environment. *Long Range Planning* 24(2): 67-74.

Chermack TJ., Lynham SA., Ruona WEA. 2001. A Review of Scenario Planning Literature. *Futures Research Quarterly* 17(2): 7-31.

Chermack TJ. 2011. *Scenario Planning in Organizations – How to Create, Use, and Assess Scenarios.* San Francisco: Berrett-Koehler.

Cornelius P., Van de Putte A., Romani M. 2005. Three Decades of Scenario Planning in Shell. *California Management Review* 48(1): 92-109.

Dye R., Sibony O., Viguerie P. 2009. Strategic planning: Three tips for 2009. *The McKinsey Quarterly* 9(1), 1-2.

Eisenhardt KM. Sull DN. 2001. Strategy as Simple Rules. *Harvard Business Review* 79(1): 106-116.

Elbanna S., Child J. 2007. Influences on strategic decision effectiveness: Development and test of an integrative model. *Strategic Management Journal* 28(4): 431-453.

Ghobadian A., O'Regan N., Thomas H., Liu, J. 2008. Formal strategic planning, operating environment, size, sector and performance. *Journal of General Management* 34(2): 1-20.

Grant RM. 2003. Strategic Planning in a Turbulent Environment: Evidence from the Oil Majors. *Strategic Management Journal* 24(6): 491-517.

Miller CC. 2008. Decisional Comprehensiveness and Firm Performance: Towards a More Complete Understanding. *Journal of Behavioral Decision Making* 21(5): 598-620.

Millet SM. 2003. The Future of Scenarios: Challenges and Opportunities. *Strategy & Leadership* 31(2): 16-24.

Moyer K. 1996. Scenario Planning at British Airways-A Case Study. *Long Range Planning* 29(2): 172-181.

Ocasio W., Joseph J. 2008. Rise and Fall- or Transformation? The Evolution of Strategic Planning at the General Electric Company 1940-2006. *Long Range Planning* 41(3): 248-272.

Phelps R., Chan C., Kapsalis SC. 2001. Does scenario planning affect performance? Two explanatory studies. *Journal of Business Research* 5(1): 223-232.

Porter ME. 1979. How Competitive Forces Shape Strategy. *Harvard Business Review* 57(2): 137-145.

Porter ME. 1980. *Competitive Advantage: Techniques for analyzing Industries and Competitors*. New York: The Free Press.

Porter ME. .1985. *Competitive Advantage: Creating and Sustaining Superior Performance*. New York: The Free Press.

Rigby D., Bilodeau B. 2007. Selecting management tools wisely. *Harvard Business Review* 85(12): 20-22.

Ringland G. 1998. *Scenario Planning: Managing for the Future*. Chichester: Wiley.

Schoemaker P. 1993. Multiple Scenario Development – Its Conceptual and Behavioral Foundation. *Strategic Management Journal* 14(3): 193-213.

Schoemaker P. 1995. Scenario Planning: A Tool for Strategic Thinking. *Sloan Management Review* 37(2): 25-40.

Schwartz P. 1996. *The Art of the Long View. Planning for the Future in an Uncertain World*. New York: Doubleday Publishing.

Shell International. 2003. *Scenarios: An Explorer's Guide*. London: Shell.

Shimizu K., Hitt MA. 2004. Strategic flexibility: Organizational preparedness to reverse ineffective strategic decisions. *Academy of Management Executive* 18(4): 44-59.

van der Heijden K. 2005. *Scenarios: The Art of Strategic Conversation*. Chichester: Wiley.

van 't Klooster SA., van Asselt, MBA. 2006. Practicing the scenario-axes technique. *Futures* 38(1): 15-30.

Verity J. 2003. Scenario Planning as a strategy technique. *European Business Journal* 15(4): 185-195.

Wack P. 1985a. Scenarios: Uncharted waters ahead. *Harvard Business Review* 63(5): 73-89.

Wack P. 1985b. Scenarios: Shooting the Rapids. *Harvard Business Review* 63(6): 139-150.

Whittington R., Cailluet L. 2008. The crafts of strategy. *Long Range Planning* 41(3): 241-247.

4. Six tools for scenario-based strategic planning and their application

CHRISTIAN BRANDS, TORSTEN WULF AND
PHILIP MEISSNER

SCENARIO-BASED STRATEGIC PLANNING

Scenario planning has often been criticized for the complexity that arises when it is grafted into a company's overall strategic planning process. To overcome this deficiency, we introduced the scenario-based approach to strategic planning in the previous chapter. This chapter explains each tool in detail, evaluates its practicability and demonstrates how executives can immediately apply the entire toolkit within their overall strategic planning process. To facilitate the application of the tools, each step is explained using a practical example from the European airline industry. Taken together, the detailed explanations that follow present a scenario-based strategic planning framework that can help companies cope with an uncertain, complex and volatile business environment.

4.1
INTRODUCING TOOLS ONE AND TWO: THE FRAMING CHECKLIST AND 360° STAKEHOLDER FEEDBACK

In the previous chapter, we introduced an approach to scenario-based strategic planning that gives managers a set of tools with which to integrate scenario planning into strategic planning. This chapter now goes on to introduce and explain the first two tools: the framing checklist and 360° stakeholder feedback.

4.1.1
THE FRAMING CHECKLIST

The first tool – the framing checklist – defines the scope of the scenario-based strategic planning project (Figure 4.1). Before plausible scenarios can be derived for a company, industry or region, analysis must first be placed within a frame of reference that stakes out the scope of the scenario development process. The overall goal of this first step is thus to create a common understanding of the scope of the relevant scenario project. To do so, five items must be defined as part of the tool: the goal of the scenario project; the strategic level of analysis; the participants in the scenario development process; the participants in the 360° stakeholder process; and the time horizon for the scenarios. Each of these items is clarified in detail in the course of this section. Reference to a scenario study regarding the future of the

FIGURE 4.1: SIX-STEP SCENARIO-BASED APPROACH TO STRATEGIC PLANNING

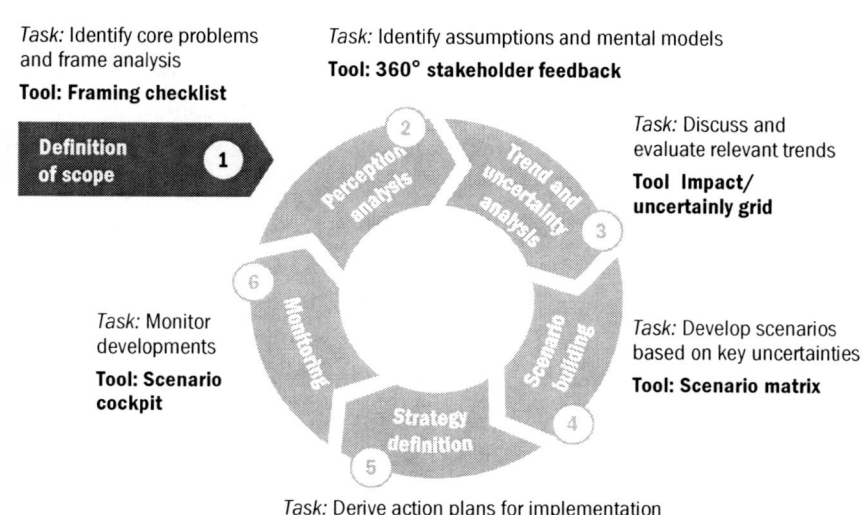

European airline industry (see section 4.2) then illustrates how the tools can be applied in practice. Before explaining the tools themselves, however, let us briefly examine why it is important for strategists to engage in adequate planning for scenario projects in order to develop precise scenarios and realistic strategic recommendations.

Each scenario-based strategic planning activity begins with the question: "Why are scenarios developed and what should be the final outcome of the process?" If the basic intention of the overall scenario development process is not specified from the outset, the overall planning activity is destined to end in disaster (Lindgren/Bandhold, 2009). Management will not understand the scenarios if they do not agree with their intended purpose. Nor will they support the implementation of strategic actions based on a scenario planning activity in whose development they had no part. Moreover, scenarios will be unrealistic if the wrong future time horizon is chosen. Hence, it is critical to start the scenario-based strategic planning activity by exhaustively defining the scope and intent of the project.

Existing scenario planning techniques often start by identifying knowledge gaps in an organization (van der Heijden et al, 2002), preparing for a project (Chermack, 2011) or tracking changes in the external environment that will have an impact on the future development of a company (Lindgren/Bandhold, 2009). Of course, all these different ways to start a scenario-based strategic planning process define the purpose of and question to be answered by a scenario project in one form or another. However, they do so in a rather vague and unstructured manner. Often, the participants in a scenario planning process are given an extensive list of the topics the scenario planning activity is attempting to cover. However, such a detailed or over-engineered document tends to confuse participants rather than clarifying the scope of the project. If participants do not understand the purpose and scope of a scenario planning activity from the outset, the project will take up too much time and too many resources and is bound to fail. It is more important to structure the discussion surrounding the scope, goal and process for the scenario planning activity than to develop an extensive, predefined project description. What the participants in scenario planning activity really need, therefore, is a brief document – ideally no more than a page – that summarizes the most important points of the scenario-based strategic planning process. We believe that the framing checklist described in the next section is capable of fulfilling these needs by providing extensive practical support from the very earliest days of a scenario planning project.

4.1.2
DESCRIPTION OF THE FRAMING CHECKLIST

The framing checklist is a comprehensive list defining the scope of a scenario project. It allows the participants in a scenario-based strategic planning activity to exhaustively consider all aspects that are necessary to make the project successful. The tool is based on the 'Problem Identification Checklist' defined by Hungenberg (2010). We took Hungenberg's initial approach and expanded it to fit the purpose

FIGURE 4.2: THE FRAMING CHECKLIST

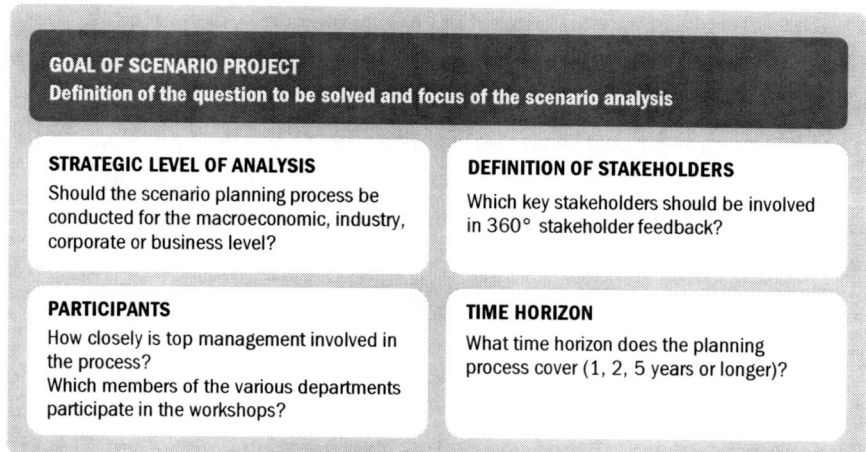

and context of a scenario-based strategic planning exercise. Overall, five different items must be checked in order to structurally define the purpose of a scenario-based strategic planning activity. These items are: the goal of the scenario project; the strategic level of analysis; the participants in the scenario development process; the participants in the 360° stakeholder process; and the time horizon for the scenarios (Figure 4.2).

GOAL OF THE SCENARIO PROJECT

The first step is to define the goal of the scenario-based strategic planning activity. This step basically describes the underlying question that the whole scenario development process is trying to solve. Essentially, the overall purpose of the scenario planning activity is defined at this stage.

Efforts to define the goal of a scenario project should thus concentrate on one principal element that sums up the purpose of the scenario project. What should be the outcome of the scenario planning activity and what should be accomplished by this outcome? In essence, to define the goal is to summarize all the items on the framing checklist.

The definition of the goal of a scenario-based strategic planning activity should conclude with a precise statement describing the overall aim of the activity. When reading the statement, both participants and outsiders to the scenario development process should immediately understand what the scope of the scenario activity is. An example of such a statement might be this: "The goal of the project is to develop scenarios for European airline network carriers between now and 2020." Participants who read this will immediately know that the purpose of the activity is to develop scenarios. They will know the scope of the scenario development exercise, i.e. the European network carrier industry. And they will also know the time frame, i.e. 2015. To summarize: Formulation of the goal of the scenario project is the core purpose of the framing checklist. To identify this overall goal, however, further analysis and coordination is necessary in collaboration with the client for the scenario planning activity.

STRATEGIC LEVEL OF ANALYSIS

Having agreed the goal of the scenario-based strategic planning activity, the next step is to define the strategic level of analysis for the project. Scenarios can be developed for various levels. From a corporate perspective, the first level is to develop scenarios for a business unit. Here, the focus of scenario development activity is to assess how future developments will affect the business unit concerned. Clearly, the scenarios thus developed will be highly specific and will take into account the specific circumstances of the unit. An example of such a focused level of analysis would be to develop scenarios for each of Lufthansa AG's different operations. Lufthansa, a German airline, has a broad range of business units such as passenger operations, cargo flights, ground handling services, technical aircraft services, and so on. Moreover, Lufthansa operates flights to various regions around the world, offering intercontinental flights under its Lufthansa brand and regional flights using the Lufthansa Regional and Germanwings brands. These activities are complemented by sharply focused operations, such as those of Austrian Airlines (a wholly owned subsidiary), which has a strong presence in Eastern Europe. Taking the business unit as the level of analysis for Lufthansa would thus mean developing scenarios for its German passenger flight operations under the Lufthansa brand, for example.

The next strategic level of analysis is the corporate level. The focus here is to assess how external developments will affect a company overall. Staying with the example of Lufthansa, this would mean developing scenarios for the entire group, including all its business units.

Another possible level of analysis is to develop future scenarios for a whole industry. In this case, the focus may vary depending on how the scenario development participants define an industry. Moreover, in a scenario development project, external influences often come from outside the industry in question. When conducting analysis on this level, it is therefore important to choose the scope of the industry wisely. For Lufthansa, this would, for example, mean creating scenarios for the global airline industry with a focus on intercontinental flights. Regional and short-distance flights would then be outside the scope of this scenario development exercise.

The highest strategic level of analysis is the macro-level. Here, a scenario development team identifies several macroeconomic indicators that could influence the economic conditions a company will face. Once again, the focus of a macro-level analysis should be chosen carefully, as teams can develop scenarios on this level not only for a company, but also for different geographic regions. A decision must therefore be taken about whether scenarios are to be developed on a global, regional or country level. Here, industry experts should be consulted as to which regional focus is most relevant given the goal of the scenario project. Where the macro-level of analysis is adopted, the final outcome of the scenarios will be to examine how various economic developments could impact a company's future performance.

One crucial difference between the various levels is the degree to which a business unit or company plays a part in the scenarios. In our experience, where a business unit or corporate level perspective is adopted, the business unit or company is itself part of the scenario description. The company thus appears in both the scenarios and the strategic recommendations derived from the scenarios. However, when an industry perspective is adopted, the company itself is not necessarily part of the scenario description and may only become relevant when strategic recommendations are developed. An industry perspective is thus also the right strategic level if the aim is to assess the impact of external developments such as technological advancements on a whole company.

Clearly, the outcome of a scenario development activity will vary greatly depending on the strategic level of analysis chosen. Scenarios for Lufthansa's German operations, where the firm faces a vast range of competitors, will be very different to scenarios for the company's intercontinental operations, a market in which it often faces little competition. When examining the various possible levels of strategic analysis, a company should therefore first return to the goal of the scenario exercise. Next, it should consider the different industries and geographic regions in which the company has a presence. Finally, it should combine both to identify the overall level that is best suited to strategic analysis. This process should be performed with care: Adopting the wrong focus can run the risk of developing scenarios that overlook important external developments.

PARTICIPANTS

The third step is to define who is in charge and who will take part in the scenario planning process. It is usually the executive management of a company that initiates the scenario-based strategic planning process in conjunction with a company's corporate development team. In our experience, each scenario project is assigned a project leader from either a firm's corporate development team or a specific business unit, such as sales. The project leader assesses when and to what degree senior management should be involved in the scenario planning process. He or she is also responsible for steering the entire project, defining key items such as duration, deadlines, workshops and the resources to be committed to the activity.

When developing scenarios, it is often not necessary to add new resources to the process. Rather, existing resources simply need to be leveraged in a more structured manner (Schwartz, 1996). Hence, the project leader must identify the relevant internal departments and individuals who should represent the organization and participate in scenario development from start to finish. If the wrong individuals are identified, the organization will not accept the outcome of the scenario-based strategic planning exercise.

DEFINITION OF STAKEHOLDERS

Once the project leader and the participants have been identified, the next step is to decide which internal and external stakeholders should be involved in 360°

stakeholder feedback. The purpose of 360° stakeholder feedback, which is explained in more detail in the next section, is to identify and challenge existing perceptions and the mental models evidenced by all participants in the planning process. This step is crucial, since it adds an external perspective to the scenario development process. To this end, internal stakeholders (such as the senior management, heads of department, etc.) and external stakeholders (such as politicians, industry associations, competitors, industry experts, etc.) are asked to participate in a two-step survey process. The aim here is to identify a comprehensive list of factors of influence that could drive and shape future developments. These stakeholders should be identified and listed right from the beginning of the scenario development process.

Looking for internal stakeholders is usually not a problem once senior management support has been given. Internal participants should hold a senior position in which they have a general overview of a company's strategy and of external influencing factors. External stakeholders can be more difficult to identify. Here, is it advisable to engage in in-depth consultations with a company's business partners, alumni and expert networks, corporate directories and the press.

Why is it important to define the external stakeholders at such an early stage? A scenario-based strategic planning process will only be successful if the appropriate external views are integrated into the scenario development process. As pointed out in the introduction, the purpose of scenarios is to engage in a structured strategic dialog about a company's future developments – many of which will often arise outside a company's internal perspective. Defining who the relevant stakeholders are helps bring these external developments into view for the company. That is why it is so important to identify the right stakeholders at the very beginning of a scenario project.

TIME HORIZON

The final step is to stake out the time horizon for the scenarios to be developed. We usually recommend a horizon of five years from the present. That is long enough to allow major external developments to materialize, but short enough for the individuals involved in the scenario development process to cope with. Moreover, most companies' regular strategic planning cycle extends five years into the future.

Having said that, the time horizon too can be influenced by the industry or geographic region in which an organization operates. Industries such as online retailing, say, are highly volatile, exposed to considerable uncertainties and prone to very rapid changes. In such a context, it would therefore make sense to adopt a shorter time horizon. Five years would probably be too vague for individuals to accept the scenarios as realistic. At the other end of the scale, investments with a payback period of 20 to 30 years are common in the oil and gas industry, for example. Here, it is advisable to work with a longer time horizon, as little of significance is likely to change within a five-year period.

The outcome of applying the framing checklist is a precise list of items to be accomplished by the scenario-based strategic planning activity. Once the checklist has been completed, it is time to start identifying relevant factors of influence by eliciting 360° stakeholder feedback.

4.1.3
360° STAKEHOLDER FEEDBACK

Having defined the scope of and overall framework for the scenario-based strategic planning project using the framing checklist in the first step, 360° stakeholder feedback now identifies and challenges the existing perceptions and mental models of all participants involved in the planning process (Figure 4.3). The overall goal of perception analysis is to identify a comprehensive list of factors of influence that could drive and shape future developments. Of particular interest in this context are what are known as 'blind spots' and 'weak signals'. Before explaining the tool itself it is therefore important to examine what factors of influence, blind spots and weak signals actually are and how they can help a company to improve scenario-based strategic planning processes.

4.1.3.1
EXISTING PERCEPTIONS, BLIND SPOTS AND WEAK SIGNALS
Companies find it hard to identify and include basic signals about future developments and challenges in their existing, often static strategic planning processes. Even the identification and processing of clearly visible future developments is often

FIGURE 4.3: SIX-STEP SCENARIO-BASED APPROACH TO STRATEGIC PLANNING

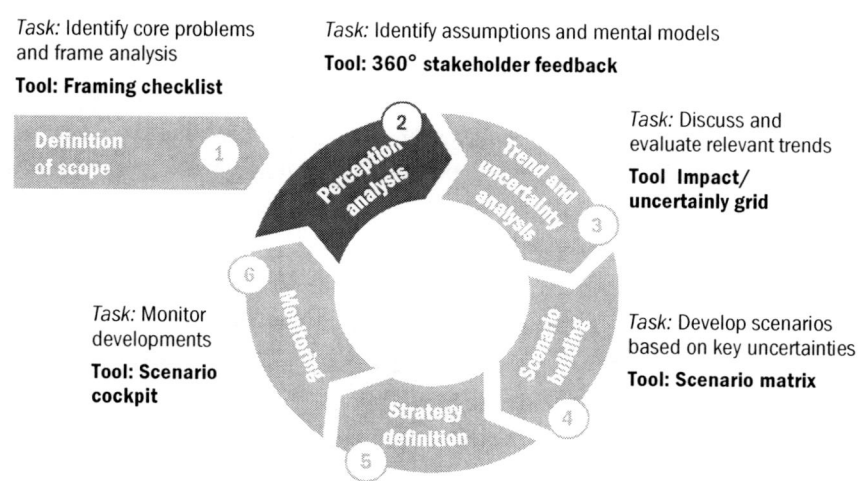

hindered by a company's ingrained mental models and perceptions (Welsch, 2010). One example could be a competitor's public announcement of plans to construct a new factory that will significantly increase an industry's production capacity and could possibly trigger a future price war. Blind spots are developments that a company knowingly or unknowingly overlooks. Weak signals can be described as initial indicators of future changes in the environment (Wulf et al., 2010).

A major task in any strategic planning process is thus to challenge existing perceptions and identify both blind spots and weak signals in order to effectively and efficiently detect future opportunities and risks at an early stage. Existing tools that identify the changes a company might face in the future, such as operational forecasting and strategic forecasting, do not tend to cope well with this task (Krystek/Moldenhauer, 2007).

Discontinuities do not suddenly emerge out of nowhere. Every discontinuity is preceded by a certain historical development and is often announced by the weak signals referred to above (Ansoff, 1975). Weak signals indicate changes in proven business models or even economic principals. They are triggered by human behavior. Humans have a basic need to communicate their intended actions, insights and findings, especially when these are used to change existing structures or systems. Other humans pick up these insights and communicate them to a wider public, gradually diluting or weakening the signals (Krampe, 1985). This form of human behavior expresses itself in a wide variety of media and via all kinds of sources. Weak signals can thus appear in or stem from the press, books, databases, the Internet, exhibitions, clients, suppliers, competitors, politicians, and so on. Strategic planning tools should therefore systematically and constantly scan both internal and external information sources in search of weak signals, blind spots and resultant discontinuities (Liebl, 2005). In other words, companies and their organizational systems require methodological support if they are to challenge existing perceptions, identify weak signals and blind spots, and then channel their findings into strategic planning processes in a structured manner via decision makers. We believe the 360° stakeholder feedback tool described in the section below is capable of completing this task.

4.1.3.2
DESCRIPTION OF 360° STAKEHOLDER FEEDBACK

360° stakeholder feedback gathers and manages weak signals and identifies blind spots. Specifically, its purpose is to compile a comprehensive list of factors that could influence a company's future, evaluate these factors according to their potential impact on performance and their degree of uncertainty, and then benchmark of the views of different stakeholder groups with regard to these factors of influence (Wulf et al., 2010). Normally, the tool comprises a two-step survey process (Figure 4.4).

In a first step, survey participants are asked open questions about the factors of influence that will shape an industry's environment now and in the future. Participants are also asked how these factors can be measured using existing indicators (Figure 4.5). The precise focus of the survey was defined in step one of our six-step scenario-based approach to strategic planning (*definition of scope*) using the framing

FIGURE 4.4: 360° STAKEHOLDER FEEDBACK PROCESS

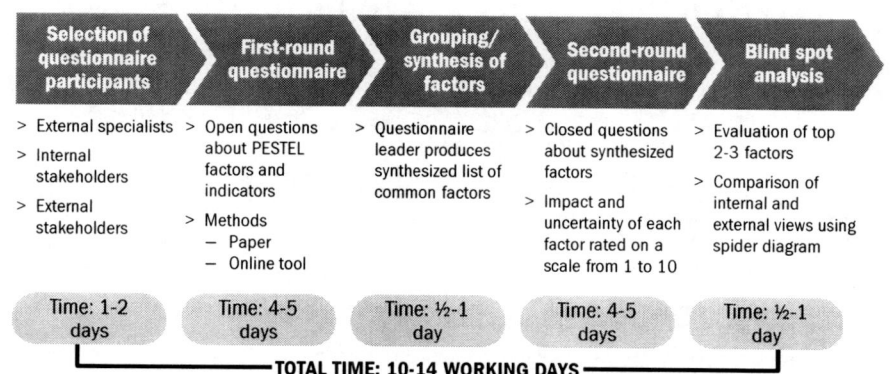

checklist. The questionnaire is structured on the basis of six dimensions: political, economic, social, technological, environmental and legal influence factors (PESTEL). Factors from the company's macro-environment are selected because they will play a key role in shaping the company's future development and usually cannot be influenced by the company itself. Upon completion of the first step, the questionnaire leader clusters and synthesizes the factors identified by all respondents in light of common features, such as the number of times a specific factor was cited.

Once the factors of influence have been grouped and synthesized, the second step is to send them out to the survey participants once again, this time in a closed questionnaire (Figure 4.6). In the second questionnaire, participants are asked to rate each factor in terms of its impact on performance and its uncertainty on a scale from one (low/weak) to ten (high/strong). Once all questionnaires have been returned, the questionnaire leader can identify those factors that have the greatest impact on performance impact and those that are the most uncertain.

One important aspect in ensuring a high quality standard – and, ultimately, the success of the 360° stakeholder feedback – is the need to select suitable

FIGURE 4.5: SCENARIO PLANNING FOR EUROPEAN AIRLINE NETWORK CARRIERS, FIRST-ROUND QUESTIONNAIRE

Scenario Planning for the European Network Carriers

1. Please name important POLITICAL FACTORS that will have crucial influence on the European network carriers within the next 5 years and think of indicators to measure the factors:
   Influence factors — Indicators

2. Please name important ECONOMIC FACTORS that will have crucial influence on the European network carriers within the next 5 years and think of indicators to measure the factors:
   Influence factors — Indicators

3. Please name important SOCIETAL FACTORS that will have crucial influence on the European network carriers within the next 5 years and think of indicators to measure the factors:
   Influence factors — Indicators

4. Please name important TECHNOLOGICAL FACTORS that will have crucial influence on the European network carriers within the next 5 years and think of indicators to measure the factors:
   Influence factors — Indicators

5. Please name important ECOLOGICAL FACTORS that will have crucial influence on the European network carriers within the next 5 years and think of indicators to measure the factors:
   Influence factors — Indicators

6. Please name important LEGAL FACTORS that will have crucial influence on the European network carriers within the next 5 years and think of indicators to measure the factors:
   Influence factors — Indicators

respondents. The questionnaire leader should therefore select a wide range of active stakeholders in the industry concerned. Internal stakeholders should include a company's key employees, such as the board of directors, senior management and the strategy team. External specialists such as market experts, scenario specialists, think tanks, consultants and research institutes should also be asked to participate in the questionnaire. Finally, external stakeholders such as key customers, suppliers, financial institutions, shareholders and even competitors should likewise take part in the questionnaire. Involving a broad variety of individuals in the tool is a challenging task. Yet it is crucial if the most important factors of influence are to be identified reliably. As we will see later on, this aspect does not necessarily prolong the process – but it does add significant value.

FIGURE 4.6: SCENARIO PLANNING FOR EUROPEAN AIRLINE NETWORK CARRIERS, SECOND-ROUND QUESTIONNAIRE

Scenario Planning for the European Network Carriers

Please rate the following factors from 1 (low/weak) to 10 (high/strong).

POLITICAL FACTORS	IMPACT	UNCERTAINTY
Geopolitical stability (e.g. war, terror, disease)		
International liberalization of air travel (e.g. open sky agreements)		
Harmonization of air traffic controls (Single European Sky)		
Governmental competition policy (e.g. subsidies, protectionist regulations)		
Taxation of air travel (e.g. VAT, kerosene)		
Political support for airport expansion		
ECONOMICAL FACTORS		
Global economic growth		
Shift of economic power towards Asia		
Prices of oil/fuel and CO2 certificates		
Capital market risks (e.g. exchange rates, interest rates, liquidity)		
Allocation of airport slots and fees		
New competitors from emerging countries		
Expansion of low-cost carriers (e.g. in terms of distances, destinations, services)		
Rising demand in emerging markets due to the growing middle class		
SOCIETAL FACTORS		
Development of corporate travel budgets		
Acceptance of airport expansion among population		
Disposable income of population		
Service/comfort/price expectations of potential customers		
TECHNOLOGICAL FACTORS		
Improvements in operational efficiency (e.g. speed, safety)		
Improvements in travel comfort (e.g. entertainment, service, noise level)		
Technological advances in video conferencing		
Technological advances in rail travel		
Development of synthetic jet fuel replacements		
ECOLOGICAL FACTORS		
Environmental consciousness of consumers		
Increasing amount of environmental regulations		
LEGAL FACTORS		
Application of the EU Emission Trading System		
Changes in collective bargaining law		
Changing safety regulations		

In the search for suitable survey respondents, the questionnaire leader can draw on a wide variety of sources. Once top management support has been given, it is usually no problem finding internal questionnaire candidates. These people should hold senior positions that give them a general overview of both the company's strategy and external factors of influence. Individuals involved purely in day-to-day operations are not ideal to answer the questionnaire due to the narrow focus of their activities.

External questionnaire candidates are more difficult to identify. External stakeholders such as customers or suppliers can be identified in company databases. Here again, the focus should be on senior managers. The press, the Internet and personal contacts are all good sources for external specialists. In our experience, however, a company's alumni and global business professional networks (such as XING or LinkedIn) are the best sources for contacting and selecting potential external questionnaire participants. Once a list has been drawn up, it is advisable for companies to maintain a database of potential questionnaire respondents for future scenario planning activities to ensure that the tool is used as efficiently as possible.

There are different ways to complete the 360° stakeholder feedback questionnaire. The traditional way is to conduct the survey on paper by mailing questionnaires to participants and having them returned in the same way upon completion. Alternatively, the same process can take place online using a standardized survey tool (such as surveymonkey or unipark). When selecting a survey method it is important to keep the scope of the scenario planning process, the time frame and available resources in mind. If a company wishes to consult external experts, the paper or online format are the most suitable methods due to both scalability and practicability considerations. Based on our experience, we generally advise clients to use an online-based questionnaire, as answers from external questionnaire respondents are normally received much faster than with the paper method. Questionnaire respondents can easily be contacted by phone or e-mail and be sent a link to the online survey. They are then free to complete the survey wherever and whenever it is most convenient. Additionally, the answers to the second (closed) questionnaire are automatically combined and evaluated if an online tool is used. This makes the process of identifying blind spots faster and simpler (see next section).

Combining the results of external and internal questionnaires is a very important exercise when trying to identify the blind spots described above. Blind spots can be brought to light by comparing the weak signals and factors of influence mentioned by survey participants from different backgrounds. Spider diagrams, for example, are one good way to quickly visualize blind spots. Blind spots are defined as those factors which external respondents believe will have a significantly greater impact or will be significantly more uncertain than internal respondents do (Figures

FIGURE 4.7: SPIDER DIAGRAM OF THE EUROPEAN AIRLINE SCENARIO – IMPACT: EXTERNAL VERSUS INTERNAL VIEW

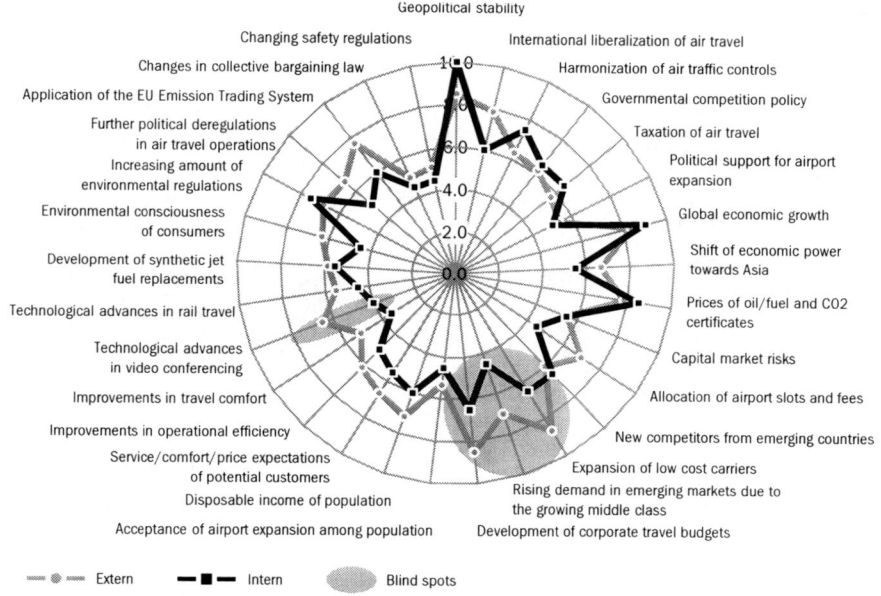

4.7 and 4.8). Based on the blind spots highlighted by a spider diagram, relevant factors of influence that a company has so far neglected can be taken into account in the ongoing scenario-based strategic planning process.

4.1.4
EVALUATION OF THE FRAMING CHECKLIST AND 360° STAKEHOLDER FEEDBACK

The framing checklist is an efficient and precise starting point from which to initiate and structure a scenario-based strategic planning process. Its core advantage is its intuitive and comprehensive set of items, all of which are important when

FIGURE 4.8: SPIDER DIAGRAM OF THE EUROPEAN AIRLINE SCENARIO – UNCERTAINTY: EXTERNAL VERSUS INTERNAL VIEW

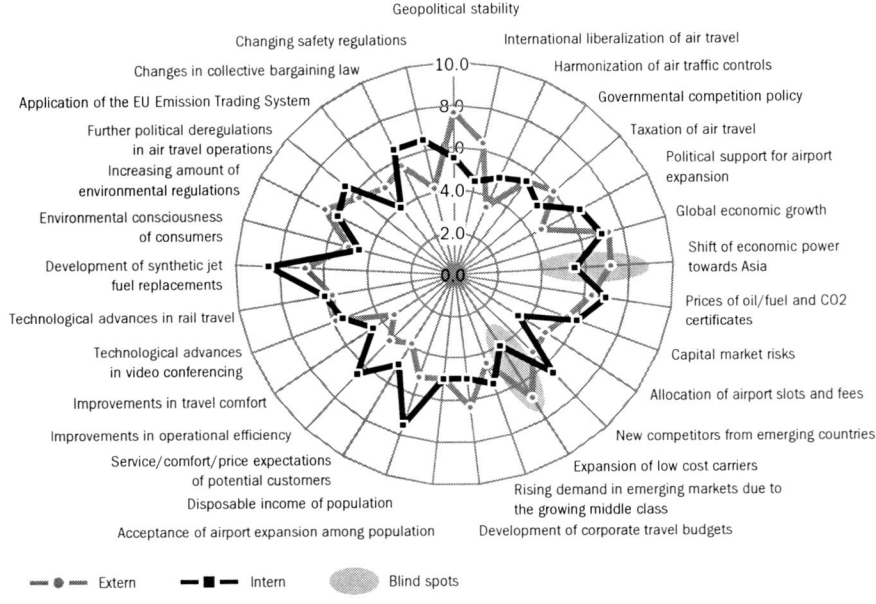

defining the purpose and agenda of a scenario planning activity. The tool has already been extensively applied in numerous scenario-based strategic planning projects. Its usefulness is illustrated by the practical case of the European airline industry.

At the same time, our experience of applying the tool has also highlighted certain manageable limitations. First, the five items that structure the scenario development process are not exhaustive. Depending on the context for the scenario development process, other items such as cost, deadlines and resources may have to be added to the list. This can be done quickly, however, simply by noting the relevant items on the list. Second, if a company has several different business units with a presence in different geographical regions, it will not be enough to use only one framing checklist for the overall scenario-based strategy development process. In such cases, the tool must be applied separately to each business unit to enable the scenario development process to be managed effectively.

The main advantage of 360° stakeholder feedback lies in its standardized, efficient approach to identifying blind spots and weak signals. Standardized documentation means that few resources are required for a process that is already fast and straightforward. It should take only one person one working day to identify a significant number of relevant questionnaire respondents. The standard questionnaires can then be dispatched quickly, allowing the first part of the two-step process to be completed within a week. Handling the synthesis, grouping the factors of influence and preparing and circulating the second questionnaire takes another working day. Ideally, the whole process could thus be completed within two weeks. During this time, two working days will be spent managing the survey process. The remaining time is available for other tasks in the six-step scenario-based approach to strategic planning. The manpower and resources required to apply the 360° stakeholder feedback tool are therefore marginal. Additionally, our practical experience in applying the tool shows that group bias can be avoided and existing perceptions overcome by using a wide range of questionnaire respondents.

Applying the tool also revealed certain shortcomings. One is that the interpretation and grouping of factors of influence resulting from the first-round questionnaire can be subjective. There is also the danger of selecting unsuitable questionnaire participants who are not involved in a company's strategic planning processes. To a certain extent, answers supplied by unsuitable participants can distort the overall list of factors of influence. Finally, given the complex nature of the tool, it may quite simply not be possible to fully identify all factors of influence. All these drawbacks can nevertheless be kept within manageable limits, for example by using several questionnaire leaders to group the factors of influence and thereby minimize subjectivity. Another option is to define specific criteria to reduce the possibility of selecting unsuitable questionnaire respondents.

The outcome of the framing checklist should be a precise set of items to start and guide the scenario development process. Ideally, a structured, strategic dialog should be initiated in order to develop not only the scenarios themselves, but also the overall process and the resultant strategic recommendations. As Peter Schwartz (1996) puts it: "You cannot create scenarios from recipes – but you can practice creating scenarios." The overall outcome of 360° stakeholder feedback is an extensive, validated list of those factors that could have an impact on a company, plus a structured list of identified blind spots and weak signals. Nonetheless, there can never be a guarantee that the process will always identify all weak signals and/or blind spots. On the other hand, some projected developments may never materialize at all. From a company's perspective, this is a very positive signal as it indicates that its strategic early-warning systems seem to be working well.

4.2 APPLYING FRAMEWORKS ONE AND TWO: THE FRAMING CHECKLIST AND 360° STAKEHOLDER FEEDBACK IN THE EUROPEAN AIRLINE INDUSTRY

4.2.1 INTRODUCTION

Now that we have described the framing checklist and 360° stakeholder feedback, this section shows how these methods can be applied in corporate practice based on an example from the European airline industry. The example is taken from a scenario project conducted jointly by HHL Leipzig Graduate School of Management and Roland Berger Strategy Consultants in which the scenario-based strategic planning approach was used to analyze the industry.

Dynamic changes have given rise to a high degree of uncertainty in the airline industry. Air travel has lost its status as the costly privilege of a select few. Instead, in today's globalized economy, it has become a necessity. On the one hand, this generates enormous growth potential as airlines seek to satisfy increasing demand for global air travel. On the other hand, it also creates challenges.

New technologies, vanishing economic barriers and deregulation are driving prices down and leading to the commoditization of air transport. The emergence of low-cost European airlines such as Ryanair, easyJet and Air Berlin has supported this development. Traditional, state-owned network carriers thus have to face new competitors that are smaller, very flexible and have access to almost every country in Europe. Further challenges to the airline industry are rooted in growing environmental awareness and how this is affecting patterns of consumption. Two further threats arise from the industry's heavy dependency on overall economic development on the one hand and oil as the basis for kerosene costs on the other.

Scenario-based planning was applied to help managers in the industry plan reliably and overcome these challenges even in the face of such volatile conditions.

4.2.2
THE FRAMING CHECKLIST

To kick off the scenario project, we conducted a short workshop with the project team and project partners in which we applied the framing checklist to set the scope for the entire project. It became apparent that the five questions did indeed cover all the core issues that needed to be considered before the start of the project. This gave us certainty that every important aspect was covered and that all project partners shared a common understanding of the steps ahead.

First, we defined the development of industry scenarios for the European airline industry between now and 2017 as the *goal of the scenario project*. Like most industries today, the airline industry is very diverse, comprising multiple segments that are influenced by different factors. We therefore needed to focus our analysis on one segment to ensure sound results and account for the interdependencies that exist between the various segments. Accordingly, we focused specifically on the passenger transportation segment for traditional network carriers. Cargo carriers and low-cost airlines were excluded from the scenario analysis.

Since the scenarios were to be created for an industry, we defined a composite *strategic level of analysis* that covered both macro-level factors and industry-specific developments. Furthermore, we concentrated on the corporate level to derive strategic recommendations for the strategy manual.

A further key step in the first process step is the *definition of stakeholders*. The goal is to identify a broad range of stakeholder groups that are important to the industry and that are to be specified in greater detail in the 360° stakeholder feedback exercise. For the purposes of our project, we agreed on six main stakeholder groups: executives from European airlines, external industry experts representing the research and political communities, industry consultants, bank analysts and airline customers.

Next, we determined the roles of the project *participants*, set a time line for the whole project and fixed dates for the important meetings at which the scenarios and strategy recommendations were to be discussed.

The final step was to set the *time horizon* for the analysis to five years to mirror the typical planning cycle in this industry.

Having defined the scope and outlined the most important project characteristics, we were able to start the actual scenario analysis based on a common understanding shared by all participants.

4.2.3
360° STAKEHOLDER FEEDBACK

In the second step of our scenario project for the European airline industry, we applied the 360° stakeholder feedback tool to analyze which factors of influence are most important to the industry. In addition, we were able to identify industry executives' blind spots by examining their assumptions and underlying mental models and comparing them with those of external stakeholders. To gather 360° stakeholder feedback, we adhered to the tool's three-step process: selecting the relevant stakeholders, conducting the inquiry and finally analyzing the results.

STEP 1: SELECTION OF STAKEHOLDERS

Together with our project partners, we selected 44 internal and external stakeholders to be included in the process. The internal view of the industry was provided by several major European airlines in the network carrier segment, which together accounted for more than 40% of total sales revenues in the European airline industry. External experts were identified based on their influence on and knowledge of the industry. Politicians at both the German and European levels were included in the process, for example, as were airport executives. Furthermore, research institutions such as the German Aerospace Center (DLR) and industry associations such as the International Air Transport Association (IATA) were identified as important stakeholders for the industry.

These industry specialists were supplemented by experts from outside the industry to ensure that a complete picture of all relevant factors was obtained. We selected various bank analysts who cover the industry, for example, as well as including a client perspective from both the business and leisure travel segments.

STEP 2: STAKEHOLDER INQUIRY

The survey we conducted was designed to deliver as complete a picture as possible of the relevant political, economical, environmental, social and technological factors that influence the European airline industry. To this end, we first circulated an open questionnaire to give study participants the opportunity to name whatever factors they considered to be particularly important for the development of the industry over the next five years. We used both paper questionnaires and an online tool supported by e-mail to make the process as convenient as possible for the experts concerned. In every survey, one of the biggest challenges is achieving a high response rate. Where experts are asked to participate, the challenge is even greater. In the interests of obtaining 360° stakeholder feedback, it has thus proven very effective to first call the identified experts and inform them about the scenario project, the procedure and the time it would take them to fill out the questionnaire.

The factors of influence identified by experts were then analyzed and clustered in the various dimensions. This analysis looked at all factors that generally had the same meaning but were formulated in slightly different ways. These were then combined to form a single factor that integrated the others without changing their meaning. For example, we clustered the factors "geopolitical events such as terrorist attacks or pandemics" and "international political stability" to form the political factor "geopolitical stability". Furthermore, we calculated the frequency of each factor and found that some factors were identified by almost every expert, whereas others were named only by one or very few participants. This analysis is important to ensure that factors beyond the perception of the majority of experts are also channeled into the second round, in order to potentially identify weak signals. To comprehensively account for these factors, we included 23 of the most frequently mentioned factors and 5 potential weak signals in the second questionnaire. In total, 28 factors were included in the second round.

In this second step, the grouped and synthesized factors of influence were again circulated to the industry experts, this time in a closed questionnaire (Figure 4.9). On a scale from one (low/weak) to ten (high/strong), participants in the second round were asked to rate each factor in terms of its potential impact on the industry and its degree of uncertainty. The majority of questionnaires were returned to us within seven days, enabling us to start the analysis phase in which we identified the most relevant factors for the industry as well as important blind spots and weak signals.

STEP 3: RESULT ANALYSIS:

In the last step of the 360° stakeholder feedback exercise, we analyzed the final results from the two surveys involving industry experts, who produced an extensive list of 28 factors of influence with regard to weak signals and blind spots. These ranged from the "shift of economic power to Asia" to the "importance of European low-cost carriers".

To identify blind spots, we aggregated the ratings supplied by all external and internal experts and mapped them using a spider diagram (Figures 4.10 and 4.11) that visualizes the perceptions of the different stakeholder groups. Several blind spots were identified, especially regarding the impact of the potential "expansion of low-cost carriers", "the development of corporate travel budgets", "rising demand in emerging countries" and "international liberalization of air travel". In addition, the factor "shift of economic power to Asia" emerged as a blind spot in the dimension uncertainty.

FIGURE 4.9: SECOND-ROUND QUESTIONNAIRE

Scenario Planning for the European Network Carriers

Please rate the following factors from 1 (low/weak) to 10 (high/strong).

POLITICAL FACTORS	IMPACT	UNCERTAINTY
Geopolitical stability (e.g. war, terror, disease)		
International liberalization of air travel (e.g. open sky agreements		
Harmonization of air traffic controls (Single European Sky)		
Governmental competition policy (e.g. subsidies, protectionist regulations)		
Taxation of air travel (e.g. VAT, kerosene)		
Political support for airport expansion		
ECONOMICAL FACTORS		
Global economic growth		
Shift of economic power towards Asia		
Prices of oil/fuel and CO_2 certificates		
Capital market risks (e.g. exchange rates, interest rates, liquidity)		
Allocation of airport slots and fees		
New competitors from emerging countries		
Expansion of low-cost carriers (e.g. in terms of distances, destinations, services)		
Rising demand in emerging markets due to the growing middle class		
SOCIETAL FACTORS		
Development of corporate travel budgets		
Acceptance of airport expansion among population		
Disposable income of population		
Service/comfort/price expectations of potential customers		
TECHNOLOGICAL FACTORS		
Improvements in operational efficiency (e.g. speed, safety)		
Improvements in travel comfort (e.g. entertainment, service, noise level)		
Technological advances in video conferencing		
Technological advances in rail travel		
Development of synthetic jet fuel replacements		
ECOLOGICAL FACTORS		
Environmental consciousness of consumers		
Increasing amount of environmental regulations		
LEGAL FACTORS		
Application of the EU Emission Trading System		
Changes in collective bargaining law		
Changing safety regulations		

Internal and external stakeholders attached a significantly different weighting to two factors – "international liberalization of air travel" and "the expansion of low-cost carriers" – in both dimensions, impact and uncertainty. The blind spots do not imply that either the internal or the external partners were right or wrong in their assessment. Rather, the main benefit of blind spot analysis is to discuss and question the perception of executives.

FIGURE 4.10: BLIND SPOTS IN THE IMPACT DIMENSION

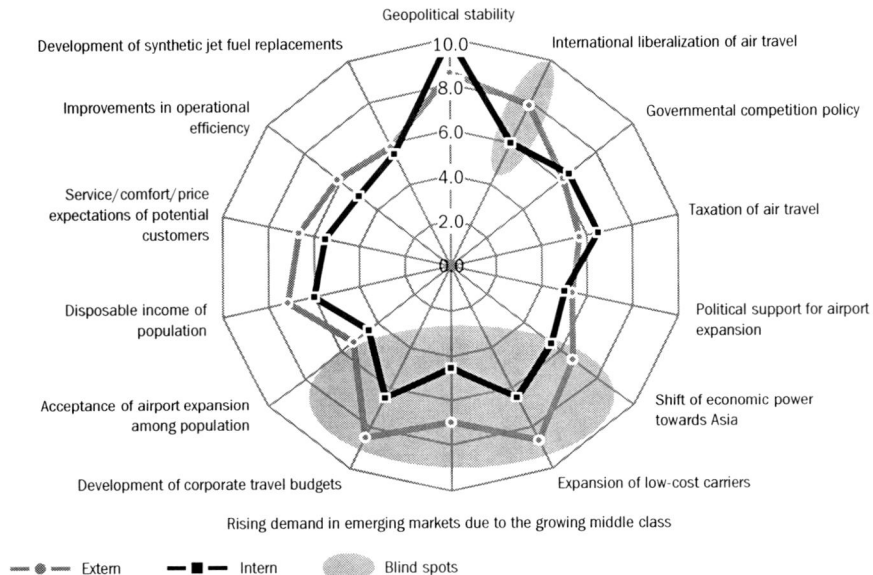

We used these findings in a workshop with the project partners in which we discussed all factors and focused especially on the blind spots identified. Participants were surprised that there were such major differences in perceptions, especially with regard to "the expansion of low-cost carriers" and "the international liberalization of air travel". Inclusion of a third factor, "rising demand in emerging markets", quickly moved the discussion toward a reassessment of the competitive threats posed by low-cost carriers and new growth opportunities in Asia. It was quickly decided to place more emphasize on analyzing these factors and give them more thorough consideration in the subsequent steps of scenario analysis, especially in the strategy development phase.

FIGURE 4.11: BLIND SPOTS IN THE UNCERTAINTY DIMENSION

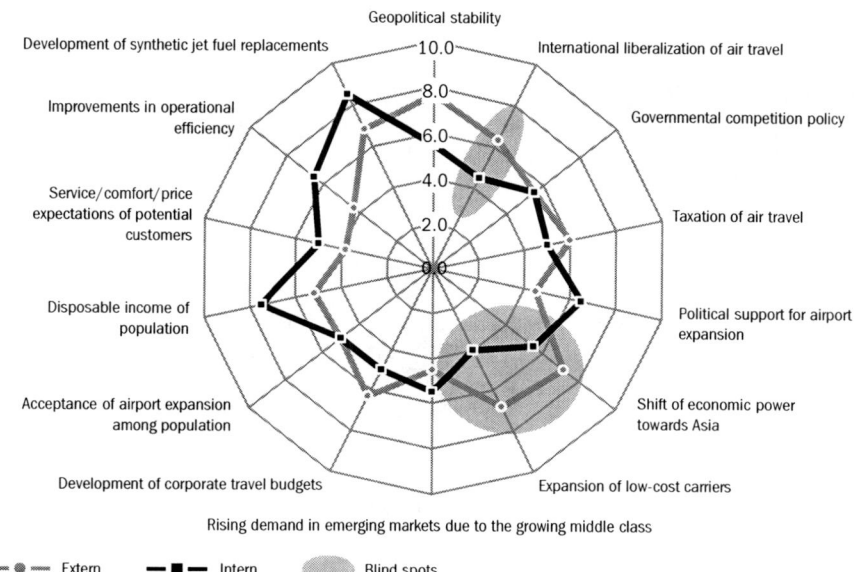

Besides identifying blind spots, we also conducted a weak signal analysis. Surprisingly, we found no weak signals at all for the industry. This means that none of the factors named by only a small percentage of participants in the first round of the survey were rated high in terms of impact and uncertainty by all the experts in the second round. This is a good sign, as it implies that all relevant factors for the industry's future are perceived by internal and external stakeholders alike, and that no important developments have been disregarded.

360° stakeholder feedback showed that European network carriers will face future challenges for which they are not yet fully prepared. Thanks to the support provided by this tool, they can now channel these factors of influence into their strategic planning processes. In addition, 360° stakeholder feedback produced a comprehensive list of evaluated factors. This list formed the basis for further analyses in the trend and uncertainty analysis. This third process step and the scenario matrix tool used in the scenario-building process are described in the section that follows.

4.3 INTRODUCING TOOLS THREE AND FOUR: THE IMPACT/UNCERTAINTY GRID AND THE SCENARIO MATRIX

The section above introduces the first two tools, the framing checklist and 360° stakeholder feedback, in our scenario-based approach to strategic planning. An example from the European airline industry illustrates how these tools can be applied. This section introduces the next two tools: the impact/uncertainty grid and the scenario matrix.

4.3.1 THE IMPACT/UNCERTAINTY GRID

The general aim of trend and uncertainty analysis is to discuss and evaluate relevant trends and critical uncertainties. In particular, critical uncertainties are analyzed to yield two key meta-categories that are needed in order to build a scenario in the fourth step (Wulf et al., 2010). Before explaining the impact/uncertainty grid itself, let us briefly examine the basic idea behind clustering and evaluating factors in scenario projects.

Scenario-based strategic planning involves coping with a wide variety of factors that can potentially be used to construct scenarios. All available factors must be filtered in terms of their logic and structure to identify the ones that are best suited to a specific scenario-based strategic planning activity (Wright/Cairns, 2011). In the past, several methods have been proposed for identifying relevant factors and clustering trends and uncertainties. These methods include:

FIGURE 4.12: THE SIX-STEP SCENARIO-BASED APPROACH TO STRATEGIC PLANNING

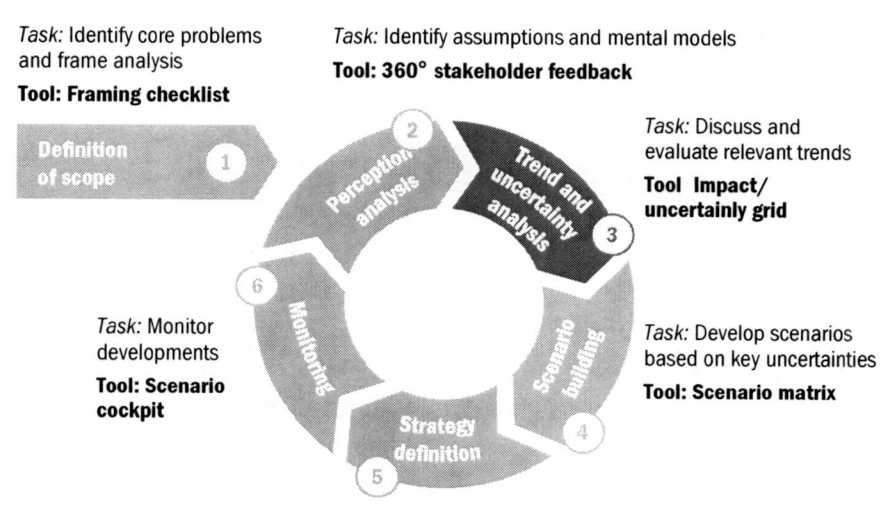

- Holding workshops with scenario and industry experts. The aim is to collect, evaluate and define relevant future trends and factors (Wrigh/Cairns, 2011)
- Conducting interviews with scenario and industry experts. The aim is to identify and evaluate trends based on expert opinions (van der Heijden, 2005)
- Building a computerized model consisting largely of a factor analysis that weights each factor against the others. This makes it possible to automatically identify the most important factors (Gausemeier et al, 2009)

All of these methods have two main advantages. First, they make it possible to isolate trends in detail by discussing them. Second, factors can be weighted quantitatively by using computerized models. These tools also have limitations, however. Conducting a series of workshops takes a lot of time and can be very resource-intensive. Moreover, the participants must be chosen very carefully in order to identify and evaluate the right trends.

The same is true of expert interviews. Interviewing a wide range of experts is time-consuming, and analysis of the interview data can be colored by the interviewer's subjective perceptions. It is also difficult to quantify the importance of trends and factors during interviews that focus on obtaining qualitative data.

Computerized models use quantitative data. However, the results often do not fit the scope of the scenario-based strategic planning project, as they lack a certain level of human interaction and analysis.

Participants in a scenario-based strategic planning project need a brief, comprehensive and straightforward tool to cluster all relevant factors. In the previous section, we introduced 360° stakeholder feedback and explained how factors can be collected and rated in terms of their level of impact and uncertainty. The impact/uncertainty grid is based on the findings of 360° stakeholder feedback. It allows the participants in a scenario planning project to intuitively identify two key uncertainty factors. These are needed in order to build sound scenarios.

4.3.2
DESCRIPTION OF THE IMPACT/UNCERTAINTY GRID

The impact/uncertainty grid is a concise cluster of relevant factors. It allows the participants in a scenario project to identify two key uncertainties that they can use to construct four distinct scenarios. In the previous step, we were able to determine and identify factors that are likely to impact the chosen scope of our scenario analysis in the future. Perception analysis allowed us to rate each factor in terms of its importance and uncertainty on a scale from one (= low/weak) to ten (= high/strong).

The impact/uncertainty grid is a matrix with two dimensions: uncertainty along the x axis and potential impact (on future performance) along the y axis (Figure 4.13). The range of the axes corresponds to the rating scale applied during application of the tool, i.e. one to ten.

FIGURE 4.13: THE IMPACT/UNCERTAINTY GRID

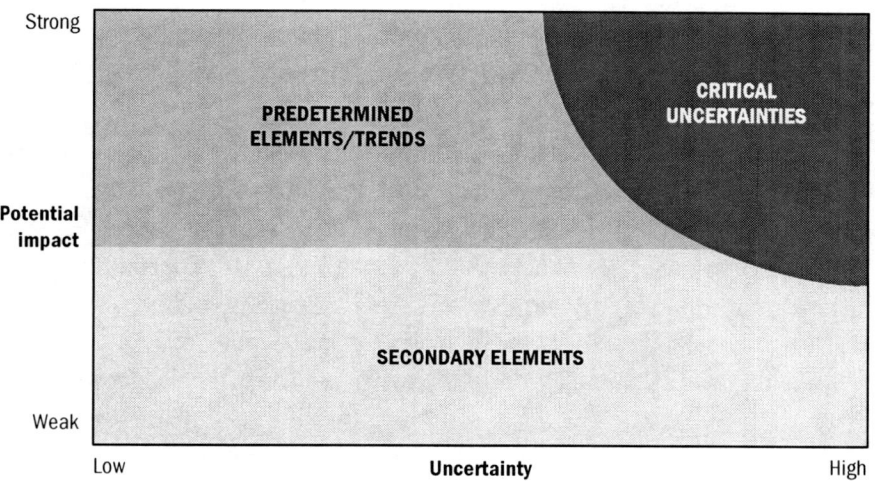

Source: van 't Klooster/van Asselt, 2006

Relevant factors are placed on the grid according to their rating. Ideally, the result will be a graph shape showing the factors spread across the whole range of the axes. If the relevant factors are clustered around one focal point, we recommend adjusting the axes accordingly. Let us, for example, assume that all relevant factors on the impact dimension score in a range from three to eight. In this case, it is possible to stretch the axis by eliminating values below three and above eight. This method does not manipulate the results, but merely enhances their (graphical) visualization.

The next step is to cluster the relevant factors into secondary elements, trends and, in particular, critical uncertainties. Secondary elements have a weak impact and can have low or high uncertainty. For the purposes of scenario development, these factors can be largely ignored, since they will have only a minor impact on a firm's future development. Instead, firms should concentrate on trends and critical uncertainties.

Trends have a strong impact and low to medium uncertainty. The future direction of these trends is fairly certain and they can have a high impact on a firm's future success. One example of such a trend is demographic change in Germany. Germany's population is getting older, the country's labor force is shrinking and people are tending to start working at a later age. The continuation of this development is relatively certain. It will have a substantial impact on how companies organize their daily operations and on their future financial performance.

Finally, critical uncertainties have a powerful impact on a firm's future success and are exposed to high uncertainty. These factors are the most important ones on the grid as they are the most difficult to manage. How a factor will develop, i.e. positively or negatively, is unknown. Yet regardless of its development, the factor will have a strong impact on a firm's financial performance. Examples are input factor prices, key markets and key technologies (such as e-mobility). For this reason, "critical uncertainties" should take priority when scenarios are developed.

Critical uncertainties are then grouped into meta-categories based on common elements or topics. Two of these meta-categories are chosen to lay the foundation for the scenario-building step. The final task of the impact/uncertainty grid is to identify these two mega-categories by revealing aspects that are common to the critical uncertainties. Several critical uncertainties have a political or regulatory aspect, for example, and should therefore be clustered in a separate meta-category.

Having explained how the impact/uncertainty grid can be used to identify two key uncertainties, the next section explains how these can be used to construct four distinct future scenarios.

4.3.3
THE SCENARIO MATRIX

The overall goal of the scenario-building step and the scenario matrix is to develop four distinct future scenarios. Of particular interest in this context is the process of deriving the scenarios from the two critical factors of influence already identified. This is done using what is known as a scenario influence diagram and a scenario

FIGURE 4.14: THE SIX-STEP SCENARIO-BASED APPROACH TO STRATEGIC PLANNING

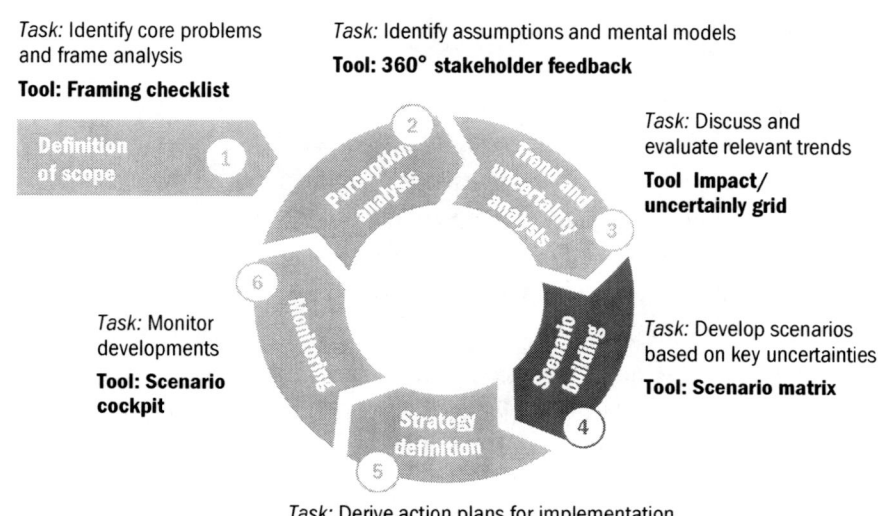

fact sheet (Wulf et al., 2010). Before explaining the scenario matrix itself, let us examine exactly what scenarios are, what the basic idea behind them is and how they can help a company to think and plan ahead.

Building sound and plausible scenarios is a challenging task that needs to follow a structured process. Before this process can begin, however, it is vital first to identify the purpose that is to be served by developing scenarios. Academics commonly distinguish between three purposes that scenarios can accomplish:
◆ First, scenarios are used as a one-time activity to predict and evaluate the outcome of a predefined strategic plan of action
◆ Second, scenarios are used as a one-time activity to support and enhance a specific strategic planning process, including related decisions

◆ Third, scenarios are used for everything from a one-time activity to an ongoing course of action within an organization's strategic planning process, thereby supporting the way in which the organization learns (Bradfield et al., 2005).

What all three purposes have in common, however, is that scenarios enable managers to be better prepared for strategic decisions, especially in times of increased volatility and uncertainty.

The scenario-building approach presented in this section can be used for all three of the purposes described above. In most cases, however, it is used for the third purpose as its holistic approach lends itself to the use of scenario planning for a company's continuous strategic planning activities. We define scenarios as a plausible description of how the future may develop based on a coherent and internally consistent set of assumptions about key relationships and driving forces (Metz et al., 2007). In the context of our approach, scenarios are not intended as forecasts or precise predictions, nor do they constitute a statement of intent about a desired future (Lindgren/Bandhold, 2009). Rather, they paint a picture or tell a story describing a possible future which, as explained in the previous paragraph, helps an organization to learn and to prepare itself for unforeseen events. As used for the purposes of this paper, scenarios provide different views on what the future might look like (van der Heijden et al., 2002). To put that another way, scenarios attempt to answer 'What if...?' questions, bringing both risks and opportunities to an organization's attention rather than concealing them (Lindgren/Bandhold, 2009). In our six-step scenario-based approach to strategic planning, scenarios actually go one step further than these by responding to 'If, then...' hypotheses. This allows strategic recommendations to be issued regarding a specific course of action to be undertaken by organizations in the four scenarios (Liebl, 2002). A detailed discussion of this aspect is provided in the section on the strategy manual.

As explained in the previous sections, scenarios examine critical uncertainties and variations thereof in addition to important known trends (van der Heijden et al., 2002). Different tools have been developed in the past to develop scenarios on the basis of both uncertainties and trends. Again, distinctions can be drawn among three different approaches to scenario building. The first uses extrapolated data analysis and trend models, assigning a specific probability of occurrence to each scenario. By consequence, this expert-led approach tends to focus on forecasting. "Expert-led" means that the planner controls the process and completes the narrowly focused scenario-building task using proprietary tools, expert judgment and historical time series data. The outcome is usually a brief document explaining the quantitative data with a short storyline for three to six scenarios (Bradfield et al., 2005).

The second approach applies both quantitative and qualitative analysis. It primarily uses intuition-based workshops and complex computer-based mathematical models to develop multiple future scenarios. It is expert-led but involves some participation by the organization's senior managers. The outcome is an extensive set of data-driven scenarios supported by a detailed storyline, plus recommendations for possible actions and their consequences (Bradfield et al., 2005).

The third approach focuses on qualitative analysis and the specific organization. Scenarios are constructed within an organization using inductive or deductive processes monitored by an experienced scenario practitioner. The outcome is a logical, qualitative and discursive described set of two to four scenarios, all of which are equally probable (Bradfield et al., 2005).

Detailed analysis of the descriptions of these three approaches shows that each one has a different agenda and objective. The first approach follows the traditional concept of strategic planning, i.e. it tries to find "the one best" strategy by assigning different probabilities to a variety of scenarios (Ansoff, 1965). Based on these probabilities, managers can feel more certain about the future and can develop and execute specific strategic actions in response to the most probable scenario. The focus is thus on obtaining better forecasts by perfecting extrapolated data analysis and/or trend models (Wack, 1985a). This approach might work well in a stable economic environment, but is very difficult to apply under volatile or uncertain conditions. Additionally, the quantified scenarios are developed by experts who have hardly any interaction with either the outside world or the decision makers who will be responsible for acting on the developed scenarios (Wack, 1985b). As with the other approaches, the outcome of this method is a document explaining

SCENARIO-BASED STRATEGIC PLANNING

the scenarios. However, since decision makers are not involved in preparing the document, they seldom feel inspired, motivated or energized by scenarios that usually describe a situation beyond the focal point of their attention.

The agenda and goal of the second approach is slightly different and, to a certain extent, tries to overcome the limitations of the forecast-oriented approach. Instead of focusing exclusively on computer-based models that try to attach a probability of occurrence to each scenario, this approach also involves workshops with senior managers to discuss the findings and scenarios obtained from computer models. Senior managers can thus gain strategic insights that go beyond what is possible if they are merely presented with a set of figures on which to develop a strategy. However, they will still find it tremendously challenging to understand the uncertainty factors and forces that drive their value chain and, hence, the developed scenarios. To put it bluntly, this approach uses someone else's model and only lets senior managers discuss the outcomes instead of thinking the issues through for themselves – a crucial discipline if strategies are to be both developed and implemented effectively (Wack, 1985b).

The third approach goes one step further by using company-internal inductive and/or deductive processes to develop scenarios. At this stage, all relevant stakeholders are engaged in the scenario development process. This also means that managers are more likely to take the resultant scenarios seriously. Scenarios do not only represent information about a specific state of the world, however, but also have to do with people's perceptions (Wack, 1985b). It follows that, if the scenario-building process is kept solely within the cosmos of the organization, there is the danger of sticking to established mindsets and ignoring previously identified uncertain factors that could have a powerful impact on the future development of the business. To avoid this pitfall, the inclusion of internal and external stakeholders would seem necessary. Only then can the philosophy of expanding one's mind and of discussing possible outcomes be factored into the scenario development process (van der Heijden, 2005).

Of these three approaches, the last one comes closest to our understanding of scenario planning. It enables all key stakeholders to advance organizational learning and helps an organization to prepare for unforeseen events. The other two approaches are either too complex or too expert-focused to be fully integrated into an organization's strategic planning process.

This brief discussion of the various scenario-building approaches shows that all three have their own shortcomings, however. All three are very resource-intensive, lack a method for identifying extreme or unforeseen events and are often difficult to incorporate in an organization's existing strategic planning activities (Lindgren/Bandhold, 2009). We believe that the tool described in the next section overcomes these shortcomings by giving extensive methodological support to the development and visualization of scenarios.

4.3.4
DESCRIPTION OF THE SCENARIO MATRIX

The scenario matrix tool described in this paper follows the matrix approach first presented by Kees van der Heijden (2005). This approach best fits our definition and perception of scenario planning. The scenario matrix is a deductive method that is useful for constructing and describing scenarios in uncertain and volatile situations. Deductive scenario methods are widely regarded as the most analytical and exhaustive ways to build scenarios from an outside-in perspective (van der Heijden, 2005).

The scenario matrix builds and visualizes four scenarios based on two key uncertainty factors. Four is regarded as the maximum number of scenarios that decision makers will be able to cope with (Wack, 1985b; van der Heijden, 2005). The scenario matrix is complemented by two other tools that are also important for scenario building: the fact sheet and the influence diagram. Overall, four sub-steps are necessary to design and describe scenarios on the basis of the scenario matrix tool.

SUB-STEP 1: IDENTIFY THE SCENARIOS
The scenario matrix – the core of scenario identification – is based on the two key uncertainty factors that were identified using the impact/uncertainty grid in step three (trend and uncertainty analysis) of our six-step scenario-based strategic

FIGURE 4.15: THE SCENARIO MATRIX

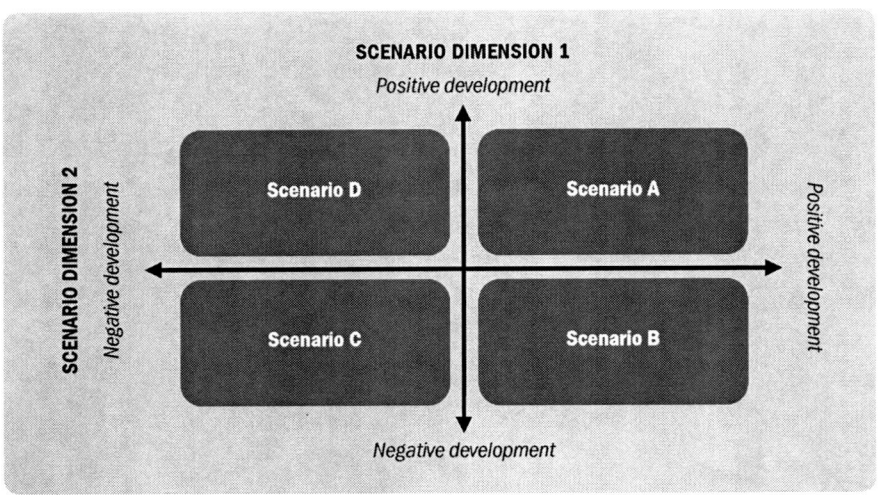

Source: van der Heijden, 2005

planning process. To construct scenarios, each key future uncertainty must be projected with an extremely positive and an extremely negative outlook onto the x and y axes of the matrix. The scenarios can then be positioned in the four quadrants of the matrix, thereby automatically generating four distinct scenarios (Figure 4.15). The two key uncertainty dimensions thus form the basis on which the four scenarios are both built and described. We commonly develop scenarios that look three to five years into the future, as this matches the typical time frame for strategic planning activities. However, the projected future time horizon should always be based on the time frame agreed in the framing checklist. Each scenario should be given a concise name that is easy to remember. When brainstorming for relevant names, one option is to refer to historical events associated with the scenarios, such as Greek mythology, for example. The scenario name should enable the reader to quickly grasp the story behind the scenario and intuitively understand the alternative worlds which the scenarios describe. Importantly, it makes sense to focus the name on the chain of causes and effects behind the scenario description – what is known as the influence diagram – rather than on its end state (van der Heijden, 2005).

FIGURE 4.16: THE INFLUENCE DIAGRAM

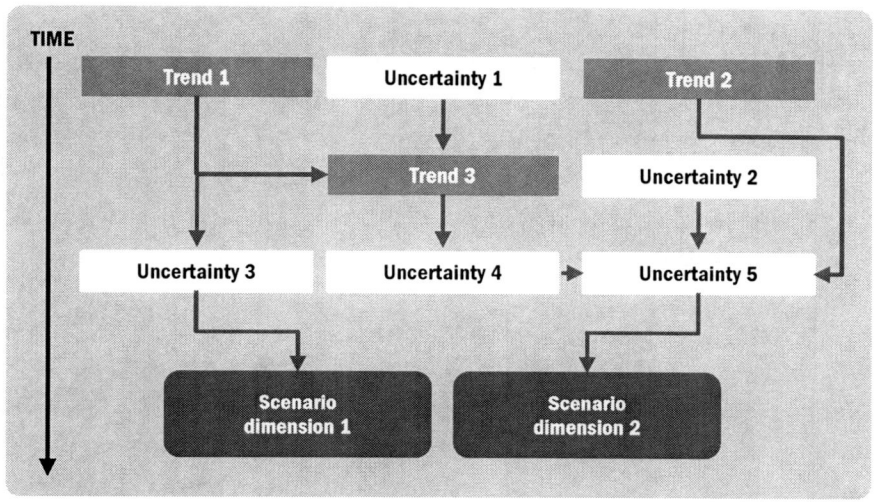

Source: van der Heijden, 2005

SUB-STEP 2: CREATE AN INFLUENCE DIAGRAM

In the second sub-step, the stories behind the scenarios must be built. These stories describe the paths along which the world will arrive at the four alternative scenarios (van der Heijden, 2005). To create these stories, we generally build a chain of causes and effects leading to the end states described by the scenarios themselves. This chain of causes and effects is called an influence diagram and describes the strategic levers behind the scenarios (van der Heijden, 2005).

To develop the influence diagram, it is necessary to establish a list of factors, forces, trends and how they interrelate. The trends and uncertainties identified in step three of our six-step process are a good starting point. It is important to select the most important factors, link them together, look for interdependencies and analyze how one development impacts another.

When visualizing different future developments using an influence diagram, it is also important to ensure that the various developments are authentic and consistent. Links between a trend and a critical uncertainty must be unambiguous, with arrows displaying the influence one development has on the other. For example, describing a future scenario in which an increase in taxes on venture capital firms leads to heavy investment in biotech start-ups would not be plausible and would discredit the whole scenario-building process. Such undesirable effects can be avoided by clearly distinguishing between developments and specific events and testing whether developments are capable of going up or down, e.g. by putting an 'increase in' in front of 'taxes' (Figure 4.16); (van der Heijden, 2005). It is thus the role of the scenario project leader to perform reality checks to test each link between trends and uncertainty factors for inconsistencies.

At this stage, it should be noted that we recommend that the development of the scenario axis and influence diagram be conducted in a workshop setting. Contributors to the workshop should be the participants identified in step one of the process using the framing checklist. Usually, these contributors consist of senior executives, industry experts and specialists involved in a company's strategic planning activities. The workshop should be facilitated by a moderator guiding participants through the steps described above. The key advantage of developing the scenarios in a workshop setting stems from the fact that all key participants are actively involved in the process of ensuring consistent and plausible scenarios.

SUB-STEP 3: DESCRIBE THE SCENARIOS
Once the influence diagram has been completed and all interdependencies have been validated, the process of describing the four scenarios in narrative prose can begin. The influence diagram should serve as the basis on which to describe the dynamic nature of each development. Systematically describing why a certain development happens and how this influences other developments lays the basis for writing the story (van der Heijden, 2005). At this stage there are two writing techniques: One is to write small text modules for each trend and uncertainty in the influence diagram. Depending on the type of scenario, these text modules may take different forms, e.g. positive development of GDP in scenario A versus stagnating GDP growth in scenario B. When these text modules have been completed, they must be placed in a logical order, as in the influence diagram itself. The various text modules must then be connected to each other. When scenarios are written using

this technique, the global or macro-perspective is normally the point of departure. From here, scenarios are then broken down to the industry or company level depending on the scope of the scenario project.

The other technique is more creative. Rather than focusing on each trend and uncertainty in the influence diagram individually, it looks at the big picture and takes the influence diagram as its point of departure. Working backward from the final outcome of the scenario, it uses the various trends and critical uncertainties to explain what has to happen in order to arrive at each final state. Given that this technique focuses on a free style of writing, there is always the danger of giving strategic recommendations rather than describing the environment of the scenarios.

Looking back at the impact/uncertainty grid at this stage, it becomes clear that our method of describing the scenarios is not a random procedure of putting together unsystematic future developments. It is rather a precise and well-structured process based on a thorough and validated set of developments for the future.

Verbal description of the scenarios can now be completed by giving each scenario a concise headline and sub-header in the manner of newspaper articles. This step helps to capture the scenario reader's attention, makes it easier to communicate the essence of each scenario and, above all, to stimulate creative thinking about future developments.

SUB-STEP 4: CREATE A FACT SHEET

The last sub-step in the 'scenario matrix' tool is to establish a brief fact sheet for each scenario. A fact sheet should contain the relevant numbers, key indicators and a brief description of each scenario. When browsing through a fact sheet, the reader should quickly understand the current situation given the scope of the scenario, the relevant measures on which it is based and what the scenario actually looks like.

After the description of the scenarios and the fact sheet have been completed, a final check should ensure whether the scenarios fulfill the purpose for which they were developed. Do the scenarios help the reader to understand and anticipate both uncertainties and risks? Have the scenarios revealed strategic opportunities of which the organization was previously unaware (Wack, 1985b)? If the answer to both questions is yes, then the scenarios should lead managers to perform certain actions based on them. If the answer to the questions is no, the scenarios are mere guesswork and should be revised.

4.3.5
EVALUATING THE IMPACT/UNCERTAINTY GRID AND THE SCENARIO MATRIX

The impact/uncertainty grid has been applied in several scenario-based strategic planning projects. It is an efficient tool for discussing and evaluating relevant trends and critical uncertainties, as evidenced by the example of the European airline industry (see next section). Its main advantages are the ease with which it allows multiple factors to be clustered and its good visualization capabilities when it comes to selecting two meta-categories for the scenario development process. The tool also helps reduce the complexity of scenario planning projects by systematically condensing important factors.

Our application of the tool has nevertheless also revealed a number of weaknesses that must be addressed. The first is related to content. Clustering all critical uncertainties into two meta-categories can be challenging if the issues are too diverse to bundle. In some cases, it may therefore be necessary to leave out one or two critical uncertainties during the clustering process. These "excluded" uncertainties must, however, be explicitly mentioned in the scenario description.

The second weakness is on the operational level. Adjusting the scales to optimize graphical visualization of the impact and uncertainty dimensions can be time-consuming. The same is true of attempts to place the different factors in the different groups. Both steps can trigger extensive debates among members of the scenario-based strategic planning team and industry experts. We therefore recommend keeping this reality check as brief as possible. A willingness to accept compromises may also be necessary.

The scenario matrix tool is a well-structured, efficient and clear-cut method for developing four scenarios supported by an influence diagram and a fact sheet. Its main advantages lie in the logical and quick way in which the scenarios are developed. Applying the tool thoroughly and extensively, as in the case of the scenario study of the European airline industry (see next section), takes about five to six person days plus the resources required for the half- to one-day long scenario workshop. Compared to other scenario development techniques, the manpower and resources required to apply the tool and develop extensive scenarios can thus only be described as marginal.

Applying the tool to the European airline industry revealed two specific shortcomings. Firstly, developing four scenarios based on two key uncertainty factors supported by an extensive list of future developments stemming from the influence diagram evidently does not guarantee that the scenarios will be complete and exhaustive. Secondly, despite establishing an influence diagram to validate the authenticity of each factor of influence, a certain danger remains that logical pitfalls might appear within the scenarios. Having said that, when applying the tool as part of the whole six-step process to scenario-based strategic planning in accordance with the specifications provided in each tool description, the risks arising from these two shortcomings appears limited and, hence, manageable.

In conclusion, the impact/uncertainty grid and scenario matrix produce a list of key uncertainties and a plausible set of four scenarios indicating how an industry might develop in the future. These four scenarios enrich the strategic planning process by stimulating creative thinking and encouraging active engagement with the future. As such, they respond to a manager's deepest concerns. If the various scenarios are to deliver further benefits, however, strategic implications for an industry or company must be derived from each scenario. Before explaining this process in more detail, let us demonstrate the practical validity of the impact/uncertainty grid and the scenario matrix by looking at an example from the European airline industry.

4.4
APPLYING FRAMEWORKS THREE AND FOUR: THE IMPACT/UNCERTAINTY GRID AND THE SCENARIO MATRIX IN THE EUROPEAN AIRLINE INDUSTRY

4.4.1
INTRODUCTION

This section shows how the impact/uncertainty grid and the scenario matrix can be applied in corporate practice based on our project for the European airline industry. In particular, this section introduces the detailed descriptions of the industry scenarios that are then used to derive strategic recommendations in the next section.

4.4.2
THE IMPACT/UNCERTAINTY GRID

Based on the results of the 360° stakeholder feedback exercise, we identified the key uncertainties and trends that were likely to impact the airline industry in the future. To do so, we applied the impact/uncertainty grid to cluster factors of influence according to their degree of impact and level of uncertainty. We placed the factors in the grid according to the scores assigned to them by the experts who took part in the 360° stakeholder feedback exercise. Next, we clustered the factors as "secondary elements", "trends" and, most importantly, "critical uncertainties" (Figure 4.17).

One particularly important task in this step was to identify the two key uncertainties that formed the basis for scenario development in the next step. To this end, we clustered three related critical uncertainties into one meta-category and two into another. These are what we call key uncertainties or scenario dimensions. The three critical uncertainties in the first scenario dimension are:
- Low-cost carrier expansion in terms of routes and services
- Economic growth
- Service/comfort/price expectation

FIGURE 4.17: IMPACT/UNCERTAINTY GRID FOR THE EUROPEAN AIRLINE INDUSTRY

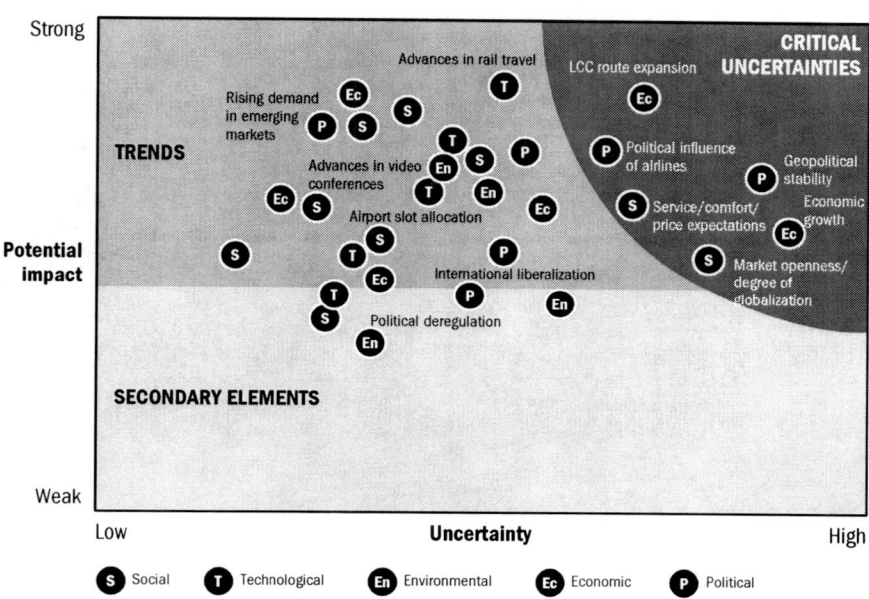

Changes in each of these factors would have a significant impact on the importance of low-cost carriers in Europe and the future of network carriers. Together, they therefore form the scenario dimension *"Price sensitivity of customer base"*.

The second scenario dimension, *"Regulation of industry in Europe"*, is a cluster consisting of two distinct critical uncertainties:
◆ Political influence of airlines
◆ Market openness/degree of globalization

These two factors not only significantly influence the relative competitive situation of European network carriers, but also the airline industry as a whole.

FIGURE 4.18: FUTURE SCENARIOS FOR THE EUROPEAN AIRLINE INDUSTRY

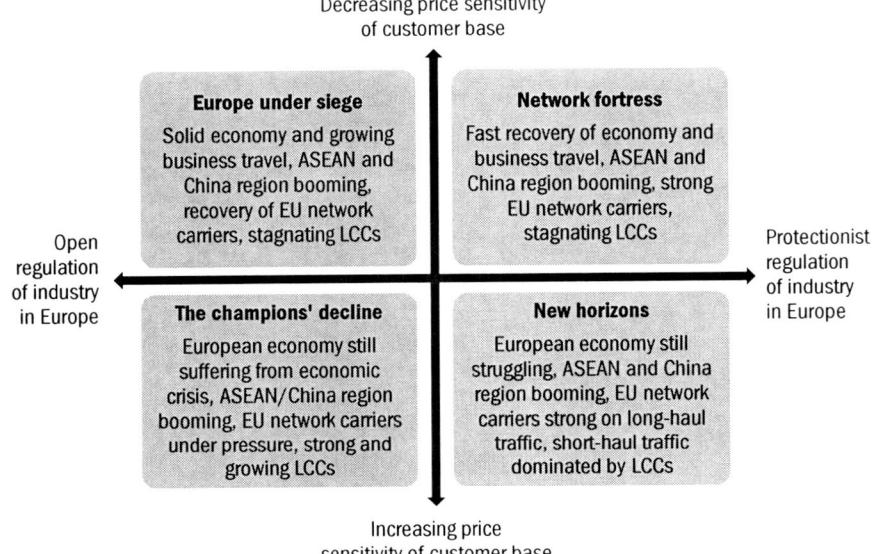

Having identified these two scenario dimensions, we continued to apply the scenario matrix to further develop the scenarios.

4.4.3
THE SCENARIO MATRIX

Based on the results obtained from the impact/uncertainty grid, we developed four industry scenarios by factoring in a more positive and a more negative development – positive and negative from the perspective of companies in the network carrier segment of the industry. In terms of the "degree of regulation of the industry in Europe", the positive development is "protectionist regulation of the industry in Europe". The negative development is "open regulation of the industry in Europe". In terms of the "price sensitivity of the customer base", the positive development is

FIGURE 4.19: SIMPLIFIED INFLUENCE DIAGRAM FOR THE EUROPEAN AIRLINE INDUSTRY

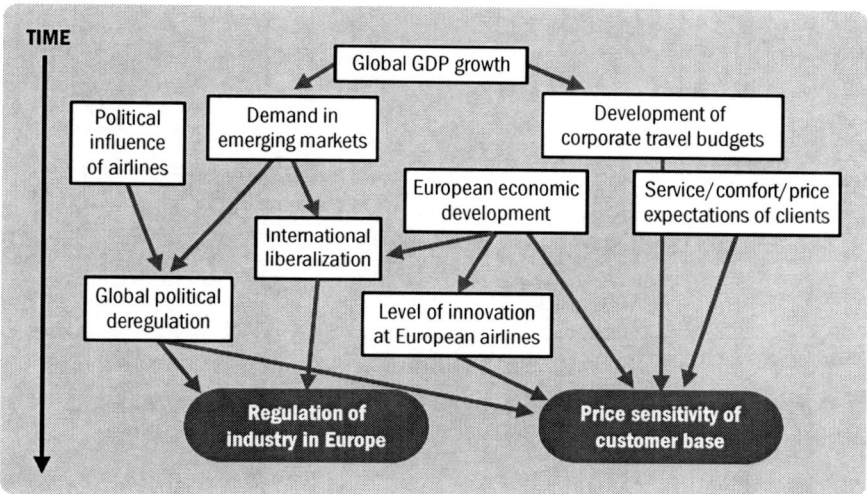

"decreasing price sensitivity of the customer base" and the negative development is "increasing price sensitivity of the customer base". Having done this, we gave each scenario a concise name that is easy to remember. The different names symbolize the various developments within the scenario. For example, "Europe under siege" tells the story of European network carriers having to deal with very open regulation of their industry while at the same time seeing its customer base become less and less price-sensitive. Due to open regulation, their home market would thus come under attack from airlines based outside Europe, whereas the market as a whole would benefit from consumers' willingness to pay more for flights (Figure 4.18).

In the next step, we created the influence diagram displaying the developments that would have to take place by 2017 for the key uncertainties to develop in one way or another. Developments included in the influence diagram were for example the "level of innovation at European airlines" and the "service/comfort/price expectations of clients" (Figure 4.19). Authenticity and consistency across the various developments was ensured. Based on these consistent developments, the scenarios were then described in detail in continuous prose.

The final step involves producing a fact sheet for each of the scenarios. The fact sheet contains relevant numbers, key indicators and a short description of the scenario.

The final outcome of applying the scenario matrix tool to the European airline industry was a set of four different but detailed industry scenarios for the period through 2017, plus a fact sheet for each scenario. The four scenarios and the corresponding fact sheets are reproduced below.

SCENARIO 1: NETWORK FORTRESS
September 8, 2017 – European network carrier stocks on five-year high

European network carriers announced record profits in the latest reporting period. According to industry experts, this development is being driven mainly by rising demand for business and first-class tickets on routes to Asia and South America. Intra-European routes too are increasingly contributing to carriers' performance. Since 2014, the low-cost carriers that used to attract so many plaudits have lost much of their market share to network carriers. Following the stabilized Eurozone economy, business customers in particular focused on convenience and quality rather than price when booking flights.

Experts see the successful restructuring of European network carriers and favorable economic developments as the main factors behind this development. The period of stability that followed the European currency crisis in 2011/2012 increased global demand for air travel. After the near bankruptcy of Greece in 2012 and growing fears of financial distress in economies such as Spain and Italy, the G20 agreed to a raft of strict global financial market regulations. These regulations stabilized the sector and laid the foundations for a global economic recovery. Starting in 2014, Europe as a whole, and especially countries such as France, Germany and the United Kingdom, were able to return to positive average GDP growth rates of 2%. This growth was driven by different industry segments, with the renewable energy sector playing a particularly important role. Early investment in this new technology paid off as Germany in particular found itself well equipped to satisfy increasing global demand for green energy. Apart from Europe itself, this demand mainly originated in Asia and South America, the global boom regions, which delivered constant growth rates close to 10%.

In addition, the European currency crisis that challenged many airlines until the end of 2012 led to a number of largely unanticipated positive long-term effects for network carriers. Dwindling revenues and profits in the sector forced the launch of restructuring programs to reduce the cost base and ensure profitability. By renegotiating wage agreements and focusing more strongly on efficiency improvement, operational excellence and innovative products and pricing, many airlines succeeded in substantially reducing their cost base without detracting from service quality. After the economic turmoil, this paid dividends as European network carriers were able to offer superior quality and service compared to their low-cost rivals, and that at competitive prices.

Having been slashed during the European currency crisis, corporate travel budgets increased again after 2013. Growing demand for business travel thus fueled strong demand for the highly profitable business and first-class services run by European network carriers. Clients increasingly demanded high quality on their travels and were less willing to sacrifice convenience for price. This gave incumbent European network carriers an edge in intra-European competition compared to low-cost carriers, which saw their market shares decline as of 2014.

At the same time, the long-haul market for air travel to and from Europe is likewise dominated by European network carriers. Fears that Asian and Middle Eastern carriers would dominate the global market, prevalent among the managers of European airlines in the early years of the decade, proved to be unfounded. Restructuring efforts enabled European network carriers not only to reduce their

SCENARIO-BASED STRATEGIC PLANNING

FIGURE 4.20: SCENARIO FACT SHEET: NETWORK FORTRESS

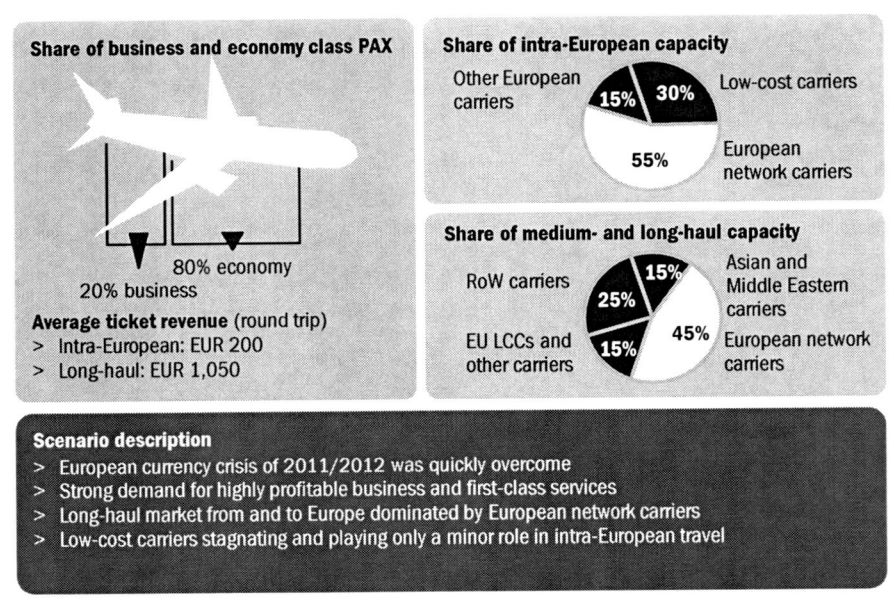

Share of business and economy class PAX
80% economy
20% business

Average ticket revenue (round trip)
> Intra-European: EUR 200
> Long-haul: EUR 1,050

Share of intra-European capacity
- Other European carriers: 15%
- Low-cost carriers: 30%
- European network carriers: 55%

Share of medium- and long-haul capacity
- RoW carriers: 25%
- Asian and Middle Eastern carriers: 15%
- EU LCCs and other carriers: 15%
- European network carriers: 45%

Scenario description
> European currency crisis of 2011/2012 was quickly overcome
> Strong demand for highly profitable business and first-class services
> Long-haul market from and to Europe dominated by European network carriers
> Low-cost carriers stagnating and playing only a minor role in intra-European travel

cost base, but also to invest more cash in improved equipment and service offerings on long-haul flights. In 2016, two of the four airlines that received five-star ratings from Skytrax were European. This strong position further enhanced the positive perception of customers, who appreciate the new service level, especially in business and first-class seats. Despite heavy investment in new aircraft and service features, Asian and Middle Eastern airlines were unable to continue their ambitious growth plans, and they did not manage to significantly expand within the European market. Today, these companies play only a minor role in the long-haul market to and from Europe, with a combined market share of 15%.

Apart from the superior service and better products offered by European network carriers, this positive development was also made possible by strict regulation of the airline industry in Europe. In 2013, the European Union announced *a revision of the "Agenda for Freedom" that was signed in 2009 and supported greater international liberalization of the airline industry. The "European Aviation Act" includes new regulations on traffic rights and airport slot allocation in Europe that strongly support European carriers and have prevented the foreign ownership of European airlines. Asian and Middle Eastern airlines therefore had to focus on other markets such as intra-Asian routes or connections to the Americas.*

Political analysts saw this step by the European Commission as the logical continuation of many previous political steps that had increased protectionism in Europe. Growing concern about Asian dominance of the world economy moved many politicians to try to protect home companies from overseas competition, particularly by focusing on ownership rights in order to prevent the loss of intellectual property.

This combination of increased protectionism on the European market, strong demand for high-quality service offerings and steady global economic growth, together with European network carriers' solid and competitive cost base has lifted the stocks of European aviation companies to record highs.

SCENARIO 2: EUROPE UNDER SIEGE
September 8, 2017 – Business travelers choose New World Alliance

The "New World Alliance" continues its unprecedented success story and intends to prolong its ambitious growth plan into the fourth year, having launched it in 2014. "Our goal is to maintain double-digit growth in terms of passenger numbers on our routes connecting Asia and Europe," the alliance's CEO says. Established network carriers in Europe are coming under enormous pressure as a result. Despite their recent accomplishments on intra-European routes, where they have been able to stifle the growth of low-cost carriers, European network carriers are yet to find a strategy that will let them compete on the long-haul market.

The dominance of the alliance on long-haul flights is rooted in the liberalization of the European airline industry coupled with the global economic power of Asia and the Middle East, which are home to most of New World's member airlines. These countries emerged from the global financial crisis of 2008/2009 as well as the European currency crisis of 2011/2012 as the world's fastest-growing regions and sparking off the development toward an "Asian century", which many Western experts had predicted even before the global crisis. However, despite strong growth in Asia and the Middle East, Europe and the US too were able to return to modest growth rates after the crisis, thanks to a combination of economic reforms and exports to Asia.

Business travel grew strongly due to the positive global economic development. Customers increasingly focused on premium services as travel budgets, which had crumbled drastically during the crisis, were gradually raised again. The founders of New World exploited this trend to establish "the world's five-star alliance" in 2015. By focusing sharply on superior service for the growing business traveler segment, the alliance –consisting of four Middle Eastern and Asian airlines – quickly gained market share by connecting Europe to the centers of global economic growth.

Having originally focused on hubs in Dubai, Singapore and Hong Kong, New World also beefed up its access to the European market in late 2014. By partnering with a large European airline, the alliance was able to further expedite its growth. Member airlines were able to safeguard their access to the attractive European market while also fully benefiting from the liberalization of the European airline industry that started in 2014. The extended open skies agreements between ASEAN, Middle Eastern countries, China and the EU was celebrated by politicians as a sign of good economic and political relations between these regions. It not only granted traffic rights to Asian and Middle Eastern airlines, but also enabled direct ownership of European airlines by foreign investors.

After this agreement was ratified, the European partner airline was acquired by one of the Asian New World members, thereby securing a central European hub for the alliance's network. The resultant new slots at other European airports were used to expand the alliance's route system within Europe thanks to the newly formed business-class-only brand New World Airlines. This created the basis for the current success of the alliance, which many experts expect to be sustainable. As one industry analyst puts it: "Other established European network carriers can hardly compete with the alliance's new fleet, its superior service offerings and its convenient connections within Europe."

Despite this fierce pressure from New World, established European network carriers still maintain a strong competitive position on intra-European routes. Business clients appreciate the quality of their offerings compared to low-cost competition and are willing to pay for this extra service. While many companies urged their employees to fly with low-cost airlines during the crisis, these clients have since returned to the business class service provided by European network carriers. The latter are also in a position to offer lower economy-class fares that have attracted many former low-cost customers. This was made possible by successful restructuring programs during and after the financial crisis that significantly reduced the cost base of European network carriers.

By contrast, low-cost carriers have not been able to maintain the pattern of growth seen in the first decade of the new millennium. They operate in the market segment that serves price-sensitive private customers, where experts expect no further growth in the coming years. The growth rates and market penetration of low-cost carriers peaked in 2013. As of 2014, however, they began to lose market share as customers were no longer willing to accept the poor service provided by budget airlines. In addition, consumers became increasingly aware of the total cost of flying low-cost and were less impressed by the heavily advertised "headline fares". When network carriers lowered their fares in economy class, they were perceived to be a genuine alternative to budget airlines. A recent consumer survey, for example, finds that the additional service these airlines offer clearly outweighs the slight price premium they charge over low-cost carriers.

Future challenges to indigenous network carriers' intra-European business could, however, be presented by New World. Many experts believe that the successful launch of this European business-class-only brand could significantly increase

FIGURE 4.21: SCENARIO FACT SHEET: EUROPE UNDER SIEGE

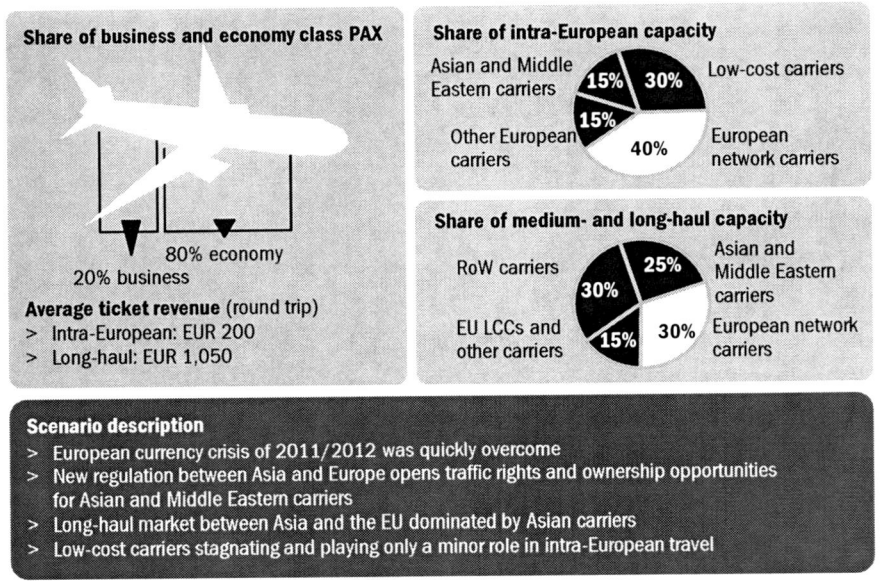

competition in the highly profitable premium segment while eroding European network carriers' market share.

New World dominates the long-haul market from and to the new boom regions in Asia and the Middle East and is stepping up the pressure on established carriers in their former home markets. Accordingly, European carriers must respond quickly before additional acquisitions or partnership agreements by New World further add to its market power in Europe.

SCENARIO 3: THE CHAMPIONS' DECLINE
September 8, 2017 – European network carriers struggle for survival

Many European network carriers are on the brink of bankruptcy. "Fierce competition from Asian competitors, stagnating economic growth in Europe and declining market shares in what used to be highly profitable business segments have substantially reduced European network carriers' cashflow and profits over the past five years," one industry analyst says. By contrast, low-cost airlines are reporting record sales. New routes and expansion to include long-haul destinations are enabling them to continually gain market share in both the business and leisure segments.

All airlines in Europe still face an extremely difficult macroeconomic environment. Contrary to economists' predictions in 2012, GDP growth has not exceeded 0.3% on average over the past five years. In some countries, such as Spain, economic performance has actually declined over the past three years. The European currency crisis of 2011/2012, which seemed to be over in 2013, persisted across Europe. Financial markets became increasingly nervous, a tendency amplified by rumors that even countries such as the US could default on their debt. Rising private and public debt levels and a lack of decisive political reforms to counteract the crisis have left European economies saddled with high unemployment and heavy indebtedness. The US too slipped into a deep recession in 2013. Company bailouts and implementation of the healthcare reform only added to the mountain of debt, leading to draconian tax increases and putting the brakes on consumption.

Adverse economic developments have put severe pressure on corporations to cut costs. This is reflected in shrinking travel budgets and a lower overall travel volume. Business trips have been reduced to a minimum. If managers travel at all, they travel low-cost. This observation lines up with the findings of a recent consumer survey, which identified a shift in the mindset of both business and leisure travelers. Today, price is by far the most important purchase criteria for both target groups. Low-cost airlines are making effective use of this development and have increased their share of the European market to 45%.

European network carriers too are trying to accommodate customers' increasing price sensitivity. Many of the intra-European routes that used to be controlled by European network carriers are now serviced by newly established low-cost subsidiaries. Yet despite such moves, network carriers are still unable to match the prices of their low-cost competitors due to their cost structures. In spite of resolute attempts to restructure, the strong influence of unions has prevented cuts in personnel expenditures and rendered structural adjustments impossible. Unit costs thus remain high in both established business lines and at the new low-cost subsidiaries.

Although the current economic situation in Europe is bleak, global GDP has still grown by 4.6% p.a., as recently announced by IMF. This growth is being driven by Asian economies. Even with lower demand from Europe and the US, China has achieved a constant double-digit growth rate, mainly based on exports to other Asian countries and a stable domestic market. This impressive growth is not limited to China, however. Economies such as Malaysia, Singapore, Vietnam and especially Indonesia are adding average growth rates of around 8% p.a. to this positive development. As European and American companies were no longer able to grow significantly in their traditional Western home markets, many increased their investments in Asia. Thanks to this heavy foreign investment and to their own rich domestic sources of raw materials, China and the ASEAN countries (Indonesia, Malaysia, the Philippines, Singapore, Thailand, Brunei, Burma, Cambodia, Laos, Vietnam) now dominate the world economy, forming a market of 1.7 billion people. That is almost twice the size of the European Union and NAFTA combined. Experts predict that the ASEAN region and China will remain the dominant and most vibrant economic zone for the decades to come.

The dominance of the emerged Asian economies is reflected in today's aviation market. Compared to European network carriers, Asian airlines are flourishing. Positive market development in Asia has enabled these companies to grow consistently and to increase investment in their service and fleet. On long-haul flights to and from Europe, they have significantly expanded their offerings, increasing their share of the European long-haul market to almost 30% by attracting former customers of European network carriers.

This development began in 2013. Backed by a steady stream of revenue from their home markets, Asian and Middle Eastern airlines lowered their prices for routes to and from Europe. Happy to gain access to the award-winning service of these airlines for comparatively low fares, customers turned their back on European network carriers. The latter responded by calling for tighter market regulation in order to defend their position in Europe.

However, the opposite happened. Due to Western economies' heavy reliance on Asian growth regions, the European Commission passed extended open skies agreements between the EU and both China and the ASEAN countries. By early 2015, European governments could no longer ignore Asian governments' call for liberalization as threats of protectionist tariffs for European exports to China steadily increased the pressure on the Commission. The agreement granted full European traffic and ownership rights to companies based in China or the ASEAN countries.

The first Asian carrier bought a European hybrid airline as soon as the open skies agreement took effect. This enabled the company to further accelerate its growth strategy in Europe.

Competitive pressure from Asian airlines is flanked – and exacerbated – by low-cost carriers that have now launched their own long-haul operations. A consortium of four European and Asian low-cost carriers founded the new "Global X Alliance" and introduced flights connecting European and Asian capitals in 2014. This move turned out to be the right step at the right time, as private customers in particular have since been using this service to treat themselves to low-cost holidays in Asia. "The growth rates have even surprised us," admits the CEO of one European low-cost carrier. "It reminds me of the days when we started short-haul flights in Europe."

Devoid of any effective means to counteract the pressure from low-cost airlines and competition from Asia and the Middle East, European network carriers are expected to be the next in line asking governments to bail them out.

FIGURE 4.22: SCENARIO FACT SHEET: THE CHAMPIONS' DECLINE

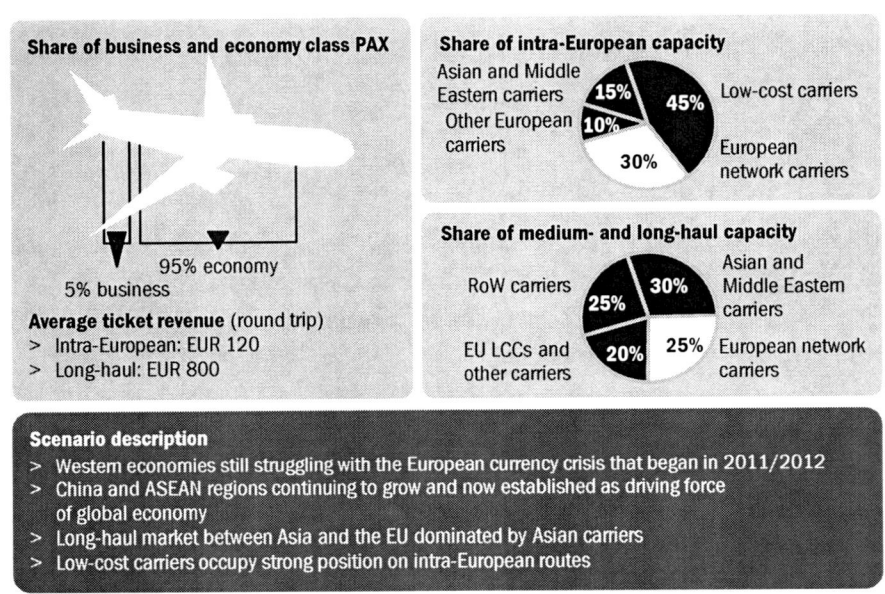

SCENARIO 4: NEW HORIZONS

September 8, 2017 – Low-cost airline launches frequent flyer and corporate program "Fly and Save More"

The launch of the frequent flyer and corporate program "Fly and Save More" marked the first low-cost carrier's response to intensified competition for business travelers on intra-European routes. Although their share of this segment is already sizeable, low-cost carriers are aiming to expand their revenues to further increase the pressure on network carriers and erode potential competitive advantages on the part of the latter. Network carriers, though extremely well positioned on the long-haul market, still have problems competing with cheaper rivals within Europe.

Low-cost airlines, once dismissed by their incumbent competitors, have turned out to be the most popular alternative for business travelers on intra-European flights. With Europe still struggling in the aftermath of the European currency crisis of 2011/2012, corporate travel budgets have been cut drastically. Bailouts for corporations and, in some cases, for governments have substantially increased the level of debt in all Western economies. The tax hikes introduced to reduce this debt have in turn slowed economic growth, which, as a result, has never risen above 1% over the past five years.

These developments drove business travelers to opt for economy instead of business class on long-haul flights and low-cost instead of network carriers on short-haul flights. Leisure travelers too have become much more sensitive to price. Now that they have less disposable income due to higher unemployment and tax rates, travelers focus on cheap fares and are less concerned about additional service offerings provided by the airlines.

In this market environment, low-cost carriers have broadened their focus to include corporate travelers and, in particular, frequent flyers. The first low-cost frequent flyer and corporate program was launched to further increase market share in this highly profitable segment. By contrast, network carriers are struggling with declining market shares as they cannot compete with the low-cost airlines on price. Despite moderate restructuring successes, their unit costs are still comparatively high as they have been unable to reduce personnel costs in particular. "In an era of high unemployment and decreasing real wages, it is our duty to fight for our colleagues. High-quality work deserves commensurate pay," explains one European network carrier union representative.

While low-cost carriers dominate the intra-European market, network carriers have at least been able to grow in the long-haul market. This has also increased the utilization of feeder connections to and from hubs. Demand for long-haul flights connecting Europe, the US, the ASEAN region and China has been growing strongly in recent years, making these routes the most attractive ones in the industry. The rise of Asia to become the global center of economic growth has continued throughout the decade, making a local presence a necessity for Western businesses. Unlike what many market observers expected back in 2012, European network carriers have been able to capture a large share of growth on routes to Asia. This has given them a strong position relative to their Asian competitors.

Strict new regulations in Europe and a growing sense of solidarity with home companies among customers paved the way to this development. In 2013, the European Commission ratified strict regulations for the European airline industry. With economic growth stagnating, protectionism was seen as possibly the best way to shield European companies from cheaper competitors around the world. As part of a raft of protectionist measures, the Commission enacted the European Aviation Act, which severely limited traffic rights for companies from outside the EU and banned minority ownership by foreign investors. Today, this step has proved to be successful, at least for European network carriers. With a market share of 45%, they occupy a strong position on the long-haul market.

Another factor determining this strong position in the long-haul market is the fact that many European customers simply prefer European airlines to Asian companies. A recent consumer study found that this purchasing behavior is mainly attributable to a growing sense of obligation to support European companies, thereby strengthening the home economy and safeguarding growth and jobs in Europe. "Growing fears of Asian dominance in the world economy and resultant job losses – which many have experienced at first hand – has nurtured a 'buy-European' attitude among many consumers," the author of the study explains.

By consequence, Asian and Middle Eastern airlines have been unable to extend their growth to the European market. Instead, they have focused investment on other markets such as the Americas and intra-Asian routes. This successful strategy has generated large profits and cashflows for the airlines and strengthened their ambition to continue to grow on a global basis. "We want to be the world's largest and most profitable airline," one Asian airline CEO said in Singapore. "We can be cheaper and offer better service than our European competitors. Liberalizing the market in Europe would thus be beneficial to customers," she adds. Experts expect growing pressure from Asian governments for a revision of the European Aviation Act in order to enable fair competition in the global aviation market.

FIGURE 4.23: SCENARIO FACT SHEET: NEW HORIZONS

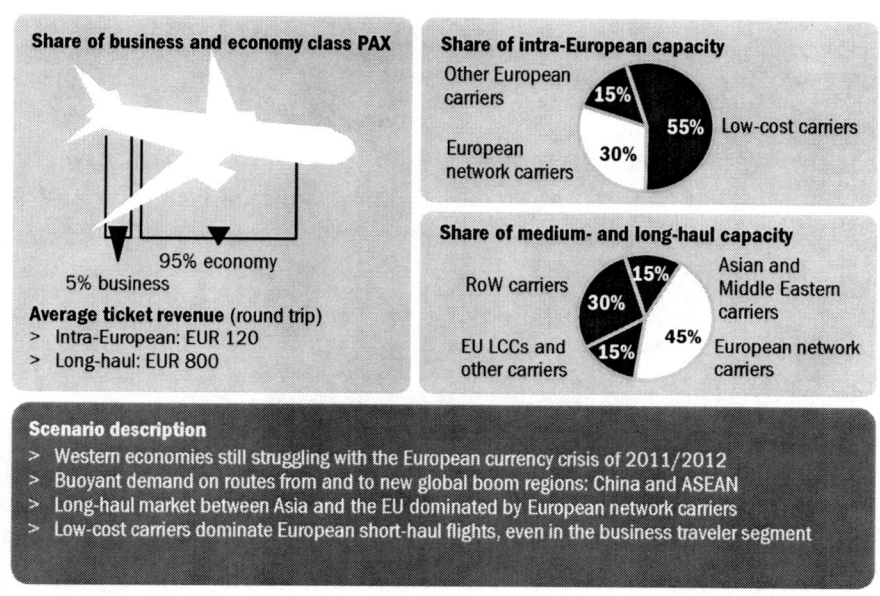

Faced with strong competition from low-cost airlines in Europe, network carriers are earning their money on the market for long-haul flights to and from the boom regions of Asia and the Middle East. However, their favorable market position is largely thanks to the protective legislation of European governments. Should Asian pressure for deregulation increase, market conditions may change drastically. European network carriers are well advised to prepare for this eventuality.

Applying the scenario matrix enabled us to generate the four concise scenarios for the airline industry in 2017 that are outlined above. These scenarios lay the foundation on which strategic options for network carriers can be derived in the next step of our approach to scenario-based strategic planning. This is the subject of the next section.

4.5
INTRODUCING TOOLS FIVE AND SIX: THE STRATEGY MANUAL AND THE MONITORING COCKPIT

4.5.1
INTRODUCTION

The following section introduces the last two tools in our scenario-based approach to strategic planning: the strategy manual and the monitoring cockpit. We use our example from the European airline industry to illustrate how these tools can be applied.

4.5.2
THE STRATEGY MANUAL

In this section, we describe the fifth stage of our six-step scenario-based approach to strategic planning: strategy definition. Having completed the scenario-building stage (stage four) using the scenario matrix, we now move on to actually drawing up a strategy. This strategy is based on four scenarios and is created with the help of the strategy manual (figure 4.24). The overall goal of this stage is to generate a core strategy for a "strategy corridor" leading to the best possible scenario outcome. Of particular interest is the actual process of developing a core strategy for the strategy corridor and specific scenario options. Before turning to the strategy manual itself, we examine what the process of strategy development actually consists of, what the basic idea behind a strategy corridor is, and how practitioners can manage four different scenarios with a single core strategy.

Strategy manuals can be used for a number of different purposes, so it is important to first identify what precise application we have in mind. Here, we recommend going back to the framing checklist introduced in the first step of our scenario-planning process, to remind all members of the scenario planning team what the purpose of the scenario-based strategic planning is. van der Heijden (2005) identifies four different applications for strategy manuals:

FIGURE 4.24: THE SIX-STEP SCENARIO-BASED APPROACH TO STRATEGIC PLANNING

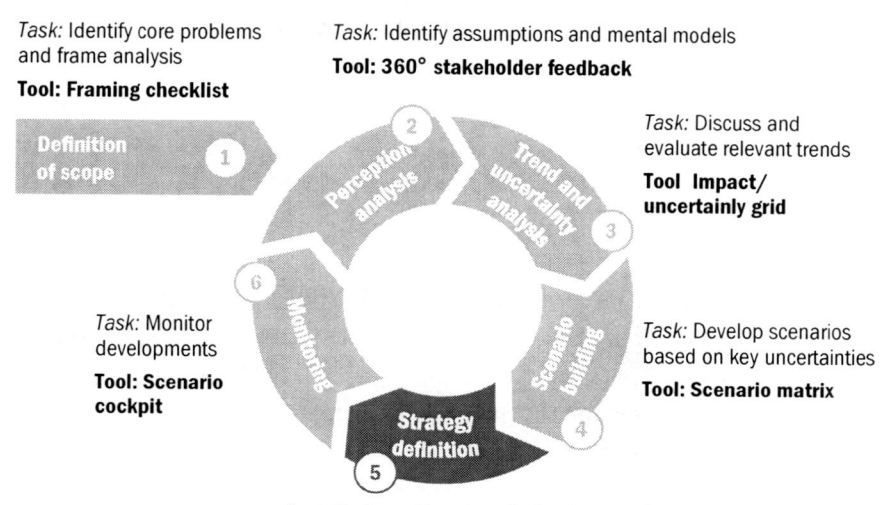

1. *Sensitivity assessment:* Testing a specific strategic decision against different scenarios.
2. *Strategy testing:* Testing an existing strategy's viability against different scenarios to identify which elements of the strategy are more relevant under which conditions.
3. *Selective scenario strategy development:* Selecting a specific scenario and aligning all the strategic elements with this scenario.
4. *Complete scenario strategy development:* Developing a unique strategy for all scenarios, whereby common elements are integrated into a single strategy that is subsequently implemented.

The first application – sensitivity assessment – is the most straightforward. In this situation, members of the scenario planning team already have a specific strategic decision in mind that they want to test against different scenarios. In our experience, using scenarios as a tool to evaluate a specific strategic decision is often only the starting point, however. Frequently it results in the strategic decision being adapted in some way to the new insights gained from the scenario exercise.

The second application – strategy testing – is slightly more complex. It is most often used to determine under which conditions an existing strategy is adequate. As before, the starting point for this approach is to take an existing strategy and fine-tune it for different scenarios. Scenario planning teams adopting this approach soon realize that the scenarios they have developed offer them new possibilities as well as unanticipated challenges. Often they find that their strategy needs to be adapted accordingly.

The third application – selective scenario strategy development – has one major shortcoming: Scenario planning teams need to select the scenario that they consider most likely. This means attaching a probability to each of the scenarios. This difficulty can be overcome by developing a core strategy for a strategy corridor, as explained further below. In this case, the different scenarios no longer require probabilities as the company will automatically strive to achieve the best possible strategic result.

The final application – complete scenario strategy development – is very thorough. However, it is also somewhat impractical as developing a strategy for each scenario requires excessive resources. Moreover, implementing a strategy that covers aspects of all scenarios is cumbersome compared to focusing on a few crucial, high-impact elements. What planners often forget is that they have, in fact, already identified these crucial elements: the two key uncertainties driven by high-impact influence factors (see stage four). This final application comes closest to our goal. The overall aim of our scenario planning process is an adapted form of complete scenario strategy development with the focus on a single core strategy and a limited number of strategic options.

Our six-step approach usually only makes sense if the aim is to develop a complete strategy manual. Using a strategy manual for shorter, more condensed forms of strategic planning, such as sensitivity assessment or strategy testing, would require excessive resources. Companies can carry out these activities more efficiently with the help of other strategy tools.

Deriving a robust strategy from four possible future scenarios is a challenging task, and one that requires a structured process. This is the most crucial – and most difficult – step in any scenario-based strategic planning activity. One of the reasons why scenario planning has never been fully accepted as a strategic planning tool is that, although it can be used to develop robust future scenarios, it does not provide managers with specific strategies that they can then implement to overcome the uncertainty inherent in any scenario-planning activity (De Wit/Meyer, 2010). Companies and strategic planners find it extremely difficult to accept multiple scenarios and develop a strategy based on different possible futures. This is especially true if probabilities are not attached to the scenarios.

The reason that we do not attach probabilities to the scenarios in our six-step approach is that we specifically want to highlight different possible developments rather than making forecasts. We believe that scenarios should stimulate creative thinking by establishing the boundaries of possible future developments. Scenario planning helps us reflect on and anticipate the uncertainties posed by future developments. It does not predict the future (Wilson, 2006).

By establishing four scenarios, the members of the scenario planning team tacitly accept that the future is uncertain. They can now focus on making appropriate strategic decisions rather than trying to guess what the future holds.

As mentioned above, creating an individual strategy for each of the four scenarios would require excessive resources. Indeed, developing a strategy that is relevant for most scenarios is unnecessary as in practice the company only wants to achieve the most positive scenario. The difference between our approach and traditional strategic planning is that we do not plan for a single strategic direction but for a strategy corridor that guides the company toward the most positive scenario (see figure 4.25).

What companies need is a core strategy that they can implement regardless of which influence factor dominates in the four scenarios. How strong the different elements in the core strategy are depends on how the company's environment develops, in other words which of the two scenario axes dominates future developments and thus which of the four scenarios is ultimately realized. The core strategy should therefore focus on the influence factors that form the two scenario axes. These two factors represent the cornerstones of the core strategy and the strategy corridor that the company strives toward. In addition to the core strategy, companies can also develop a small number of scenario-specific strategy options that are only to be implemented under certain conditions.

To summarize, the overall goal of the strategy manual is to develop a core strategy for the strategy corridor by defining focal points for the different scenario environments. These focal points, which form the boundaries of the scenarios, are those elements of the core strategy that must be more rigorously implemented than the others, depending on which scenario is realized. In addition, the strategy manual can be used to define certain scenario-specific strategy options.

4.5.3
DESCRIPTION OF THE STRATEGY MANUAL

The strategy manual presented here is based on traditional strategic planning processes (e.g. Ansoff/Nakamura, 2007; Mintzberg, 1994). We have applied it successfully as a tool in numerous scenario-based strategic planning projects. Companies can use it in their scenario planning to identify clear strategic actions for implementation. It is complemented by a strategy corridor that helps align these strategic actions with key uncertainties.

THE STRATEGY CORRIDOR
The strategy manual rests on the belief that companies always strive toward the most positive scenario. This scenario is usually located in the upper right-hand corner of the scenario matrix. Of course, in reality the company is not always able to move toward this scenario, but it remains the overall strategic goal toward which the company strives.

The first step is for the scenario planning team to agree that it wants to move toward the most positive scenario. Next, the team should analyze the factors influencing the development of the scenario in question. The two main factors are the two axes of the scenarios and their corresponding critical uncertainties. These two factors drive the development of the scenario and form the focus of the strategy corridor.

Starting with the first axis, the team members should ask themselves the following questions:
1. How can we benefit from a positive development along this axis?
2. How can we avoid or manage any negative development along this axis?

Once this is clear to the team, they can begin devising specific strategic actions aimed at maximizing positive development and minimizing negative development along the first axis. When they have done this, they should do the same for the second scenario axis. The two scenario axes together create the corridor that guides strategy development.

So far, the corridor contains only strategic actions focused on the two scenario axes. The team now needs to include the trends and other factors influencing the two axes. They can do this by using the influence diagram developed in step four of the scenario-based strategic planning process. Each factor and trend in the diagram should be transferred to the scenario matrix. This makes it clear which factors and trends drive the two axes.

Next, the team should analyze each trend and factor in detail, as they did for the two axes. Once again, they should ask themselves how they can benefit from the positive development of a trend or factor, and how they can best avoid or manage any negative development. As shown in figure 4.25, the trends and factors in the scenario matrix fill the strategy corridor and form the basis of the strategy manual.

APPLICATION OF THE STRATEGY MANUAL
Having defined the strategy corridor, the next step is to examine each trend and uncertainty in detail. The two scenario dimensions form the boundaries of the

FIGURE 4.25: THE STRATEGY CORRIDOR

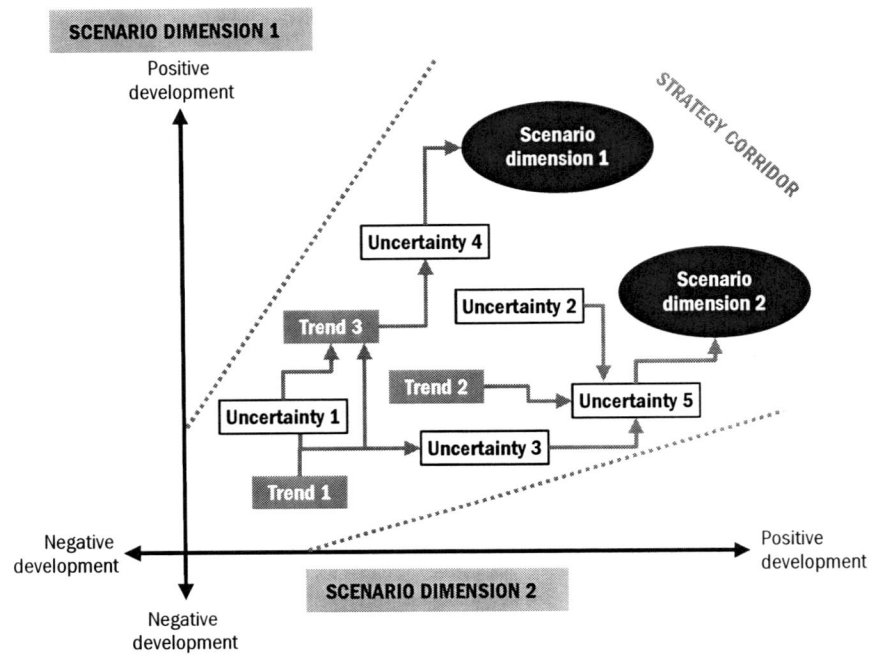

strategy manual, in the sense that they are the core elements of the strategy manual. These two scenario dimensions are shaped and influenced by the cause and effect chain represented by the links between the various trends and uncertainties. The scenario planning team thus knows which trends and uncertainties need to develop in a positive direction for a specific scenario dimension to dominate future scenarios in a positive manner. In figure 4.25, for example, trend 1 must positively influence uncertainties 3 and 5 in order for scenario dimension 2 to develop positively.

Armed with this knowledge, the team can now determine the specific strategic actions that they need to take in order to benefit from trend 1. They can do this by quantifying the relationship between the various trends, uncertainties and key business drivers. The team can also determine from uncertainties 3 and 5 which strategic actions they need to take in order to positively drive scenario dimension 2. They can then do the same for scenario dimension 1. By this means, they can develop a set of highly specific, easily managed strategic actions, which together form the core strategy.

In reality, it rarely happens that all the trends and uncertainties develop in a positive direction. The team should therefore develop, in addition to the core strategy, some scenario-specific strategic options. Again, the strategy corridor and scenario options can function as a basis for developing these strategic options. In our experience, most trends and uncertainties develop in a positive direction, with only one or two developing negatively. These one or two elements form the basis for developing the scenario-specific strategic options.

Figure 4.25 can also be used to illustrate this situation. The strategy corridor still points in a positive direction overall but it is now wider, incorporating a few trends and uncertainties that develop in a negative direction, namely trend 2 and uncertainties 3 and 5 (influencing scenario dimension 2 negatively). In this situation the company can still implement the initially envisioned core strategy but this core strategy must be supported by scenario-specific options that mitigate the negative threats posed by trend 2 and uncertainties 3 and 5. By incorporating these scenario-specific options, scenario dimension 2 remains positive overall.

In fact, the elements for which the company must develop scenario-specific options are the same as in a pure core strategy leading in a positive direction. However, the strategic actions focusing on the two scenario axes are implemented more strictly. How strictly depends on where the company is currently located along the scenario dimensions.

4.5.4
THE SCENARIO COCKPIT

In this section we describe the final stage of our six-step scenario-based approach to strategic planning: the monitoring stage. We show how a strategic controlling system indicating which strategic measures should be implemented can be set up

FIGURE 4.26: THE SIX-STEP SCENARIO-BASED APPROACH TO STRATEGIC PLANNING

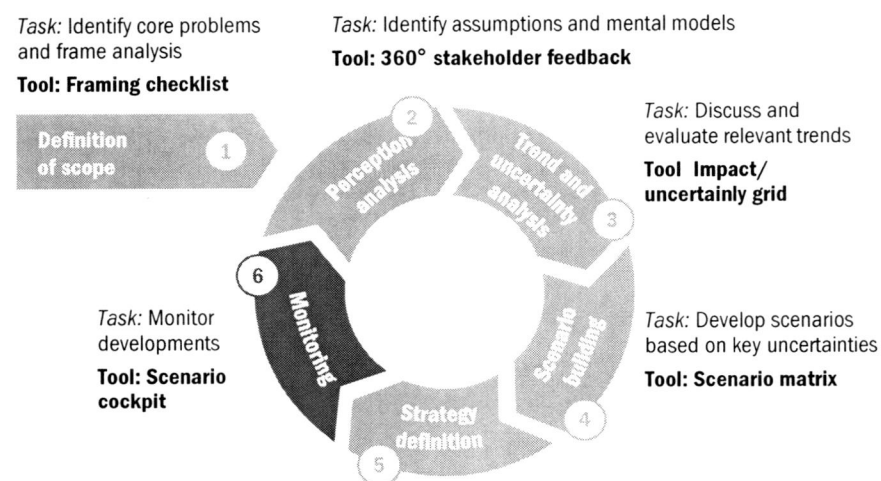

using the "scenario cockpit" tool (Figure 4.26). The overall goal of this stage is to identify which of the strategic options previously developed should be implemented and at what point in time. Of particular interest is the actual process of setting up a monitoring system to help track external developments. We also examine what elements this system should comprise. Before turning to the scenario cockpit itself, we examine what a strategic controlling process actually consists of, what the basic idea behind the tool is and how planners can monitor external developments.

Strategic controlling is important as it allows decision makers to determine which of the strategic options developed using the strategy manual should be implemented first and under what conditions. In an earlier stage of the process we developed specific strategic options to be implemented under certain conditions. Now we need to look at how the external environment is actually developing and which scenario will actually come into being. The scenario cockpit helps us do this. Based on its results, we can implement the strategic actions developed earlier or adjust them as necessary.

It is important to note that simply developing scenarios and corresponding strategic actions is not sufficient in itself. The scenario-based strategic planning process must go further, implementing a formal controlling system that allows us to monitor external developments. Strategic controlling systems enable companies to react in a flexible manner to any external changes that occur in their environment. The information that these systems produce should be passed on to senior managers on a regular basis so that they can react to these developments and implement appropriate strategic actions. It is thus important not only to monitor external developments but to link them to the scenarios developed earlier on in the process, allowing managers to concentrate on specific strategic actions within the strategy corridor (Wulf/Stubner, 2012).

Essentially, the scenario cockpit is a strategic controlling system that monitors external developments. Most scenarios are of a qualitative nature, so adding quantifications where appropriate increases the plausibility of the scenarios and facilitates the monitoring of external developments. The scenario cockpit makes this possible and is thus an essential part of our approach to scenario-based strategic planning.

4.5.5
DESCRIPTION OF THE SCENARIO COCKPIT

The scenario cockpit described in this section is an extension of a strategic controlling concept first described by Wulf and Stubner (2012). It further draws on our own experience in scenario-based strategic planning projects.

The purpose of the scenario cockpit is to monitor external developments. It is an adaptable, easy to implement system. The first step is to identify indicators for external developments. The 360° stakeholder feedback may give some pointers

FIGURE 4.27: INFLUENCE DIAGRAM

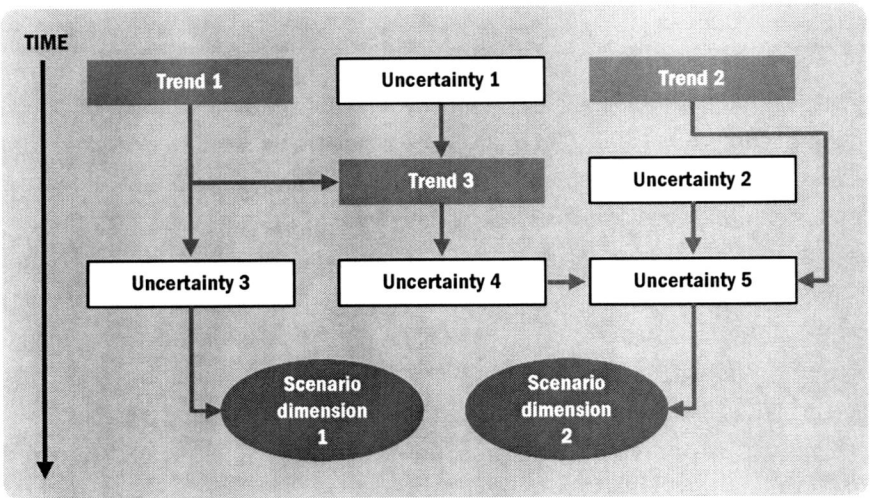

here, but a more effective way of finding indicators is to look at the influence diagram drawn up in the fourth stage of the scenario-planning process. This influence diagram is based on the results of the 360° stakeholder feedback and shows the interplay of factors needed for a certain scenario dimension to develop and lead to a specific scenario (Figure 4.27).

We therefore go back to the influence diagram and divide the influence factors into trends and critical uncertainties (see section 4.3.4). Having done this, we now determine if it is possible to attach a quantitative indicator – GDP growth, say – to each of the influence factors. This involves looking for proven actions and databases that can accurately measure developments in individual factors.

Finding quantitative indicators for trends is relatively straightforward as they have usually already been established by management research. They include OECD indicators and data from trend studies by consulting firms. Critical uncertainties are frequently more difficult to measure quantitatively. If no quantitative measures are available, qualitative measures may have to be used. Examples of such measures

FIGURE 4.28: INDICATOR TABLE

INFLUENCE FACTORS	INDICATORS
Trend 1	German GDP growth
Trend 2	Demographic age distribution
Trend 3	Percentage of revenues spent on R&D
Uncertainty 1	Customer satisfaction with new products
Uncertainty 2	No. of articles on market liberalization
Uncertainty 3	Customer demand in emerging markets
Uncertainty 4	Reform initiatives debated in parliament
Uncertainty 5	Corporate spending on video conferences

include interviews to see how customer expectations are changing and keyword searches on Google news to scan media stories.

Next, we list the influence factors and their corresponding indicators in a table (Figure 4.28). This helps us avoid using the same indicator to measure more than one influence factor, which might lead us to misinterpret developments.

The indicator table is also useful for defining the "monitoring corridor" – a value range for each indicator and scenario that allows us to see which scenario is developing. Drawing up the monitoring corridor involves defining the value range that an indicator must reach in order for a certain scenario to develop. Having defined these value ranges, we must then match them to each scenario, avoiding any overlaps.

The final step is to apply a traffic light system to the data. Here, we suggest using an Excel spreadsheet. The purpose of the traffic lights is to indicate the direction in which the external environment is moving. The different colors should be linked to a value range for each indicator, with green standing for an increase, yellow for an average value and red for a decrease. Indicators should be checked

FIGURE 4.29: SCENARIO COCKPIT: TRAFFIC LIGHT SYSTEM

	Indicator 1	Indicator 2	Indicator 3	Indicator 4
SCENARIO A	green	green	yellow	green
SCENARIO B	red	yellow	green	red
SCENARIO C	red	yellow	red	red
SCENARIO D	red	red	red	red

regularly and the colors of the traffic lights changed accordingly. Senior managers should discuss any changes and identify what lies behind them, deciding what strategic actions to take. Changes in traffic lights are easy to communicate via an e-mail alert system linked to the Excel spreadsheet (Figure 4.29).

4.5.6
EVALUATING THE STRATEGY MANUAL AND THE SCENARIO COCKPIT

The strategy manual is a quick, straightforward process for drawing up a core strategy supported by a small number of scenario-specific strategy options. Developing a strategy corridor and a core strategy increases flexibility as it allows planners to steer their company in the desired direction. Identifying common influence factors within the strategy corridor automatically points the planners toward strategic actions that they can then implement. At the same time, the strategy manual takes a holistic approach by covering all possible future developments with its specific strategies.

The strategy manual has a number of shortcomings; however, these are manageable. First, developing a core strategy and scenario-specific options for all possible elements is resource-intensive. Accordingly, companies should carefully identify which specific influence factors they lack a strategy for, and which they have already dealt with in their earlier planning activities. Second, no matter how effective the strategy manual, the future remains uncertain: Companies cannot plan for all possible future developments.

The scenario cockpit is a simple tool for monitoring external developments and identifying which of the strategic options developed earlier on in the scenario-based strategic planning process should be implemented. Using the scenario cockpit to track external developments offers a high degree of flexibility as the tool can be quickly customized to the planners' requirements. Indicators are provided by the 360° stakeholder feedback and influence diagram; they do not need to be developed from scratch. Moreover, the tool offers a holistic approach to monitoring external developments as all relevant trends and critical uncertainties are matched to qualitative or quantitative indicators. The scenario cockpit thus incorporates an automatic safety mechanism.

The scenario cockpit has certain shortcomings when applied in practice. First, matching trends and critical uncertainties to indicators can be a time-consuming task, especially in the case of qualitative indicators. Here, a carefully thought-through influence diagram reduces the amount of effort needed. Second, there is a danger that an indicator might be forgotten or neglected, leading to incomplete results or a misinterpretation of external developments. If this happens, the company could end up thinking that the world is moving in the direction of Scenario A when in fact it is moving in the direction of Scenario B. However, if the influence diagram has been developed correctly, the danger of forgetting to include an indicator in the scenario cockpit is small.

The outcome of the strategy manual and scenario cockpit is a core strategy consisting of no-regret actions that companies can implement in any scenario, plus a strategic monitoring system that allows senior managers to track external developments and implement the right strategic actions at an appropriate time. Moreover, the strategy manual delivers a set of strategic options that can be implemented in highly specific scenario conditions. The scenario cockpit also allows senior managers to adjust the strategic initiatives developed earlier in the light of external developments.

4.6 APPLYING FRAMEWORKS FIVE AND SIX: THE STRATEGY MANUAL AND THE SCENARIO COCKPIT IN THE EUROPEAN AIRLINE INDUSTRY

4.6.1 THE STRATEGY MANUAL

We recently used the strategy manual as a tool in a study of the European airline industry from the perspective of network carriers, such as Lufthansa, Air France-KLM and British Airways. The strategic recommendations presented in this section were intended as practical first steps to be taken by network carriers in general; detailed strategy recommendations would require an analysis of the current situation of the specific company in question. As discussed in earlier sections, we identified two key uncertainties in the European airline industry: *degree of regulation of the industry in Europe* and *price sensitivity of the customer base*. These two uncertainties formed the scenario dimensions which led to the following four scenarios:

Looking at the four scenarios and the influence diagram, it becomes clear that European network carriers would like to create an environment in which their industry enjoys protectionist regulation (keeping foreign competitors out of the market) and a strong economic environment where customers are less price-sensitive than today.

The first step was to examine what strategic actions could influence the uncertainty of the *degree of regulation of the industry in Europe*. The answer is that European network carriers should monitor European regulators more closely, drawing attention to the economic and social significance of their industry. In

FIGURE 4.30: SCENARIOS FOR THE EUROPEAN AIRLINE INDUSTRY

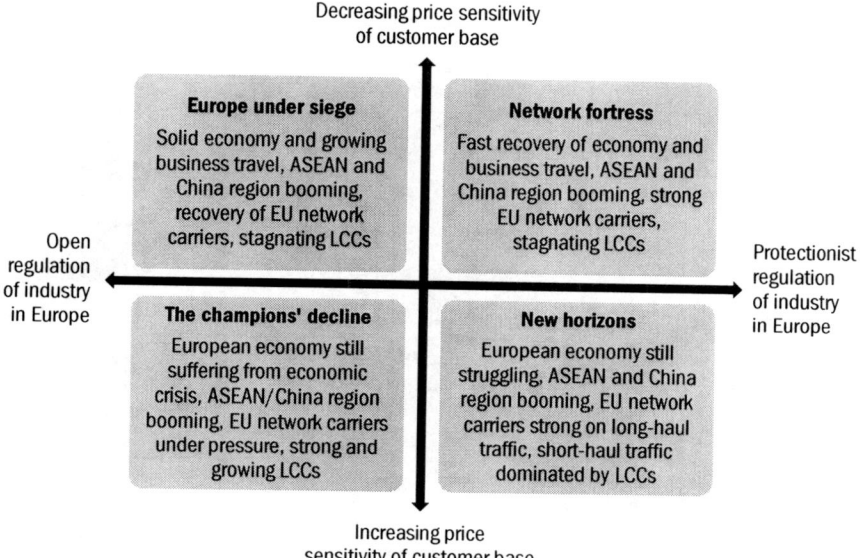

addition, they should make strategic moves that help protect their home markets whilst benefitting from trends such as the liberalization of international air travel. These strategic moves could include influencing regulators, allocating landing slots at airports and lobbying national and European bodies to reassess the opening up of markets to foreign airlines.

The second step was to determine what strategic actions would influence the uncertainty of the *price sensitivity of the customer base*. Here, European network carriers should pursue a strategy of investing in everything the customer sees, while saving costs and driving efficiency in back-office and support processes. Companies can manage both scenario axes by restructuring operations while simultaneously increasing service and quality levels to remain competitive and lobbying governing bodies to regulate markets in favor of European network carriers.

FIGURE 4.31: STRATEGY CORRIDOR FOR THE EUROPEAN AIRLINE INDUSTRY

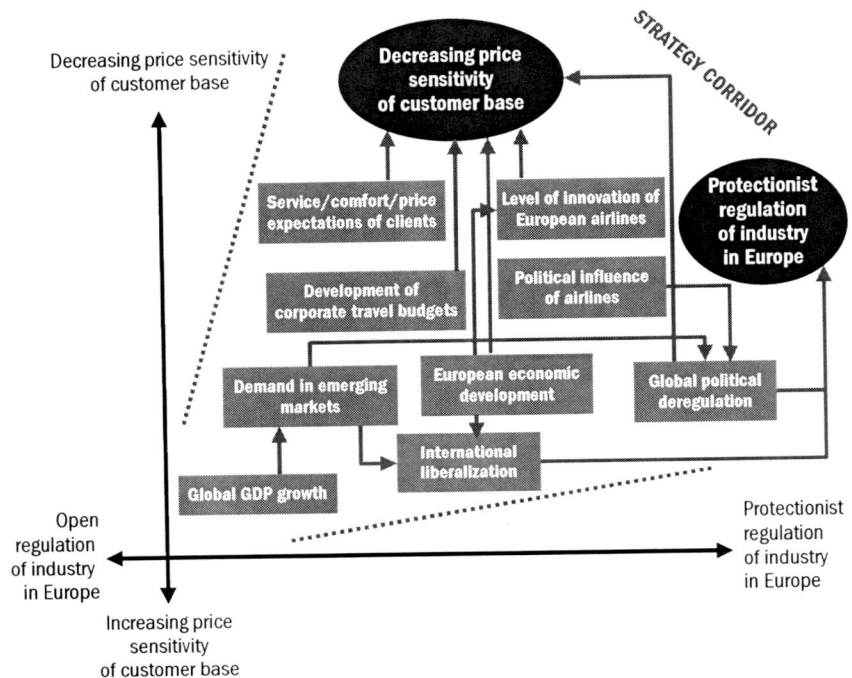

To shed further light on what drives the scenario axes and what strategic action is required, we then transferred the influence diagram to the strategy corridor. This revealed additional elements that the core strategy should contain (figure 4.31).

Next, we examined each trend and uncertainty in detail. This revealed that several of the factors that extend beyond the scenario axes are hard to influence by the network carriers – global GDP growth demand in emerging markets and European economic development, for instance. The carriers need to closely monitor these factors and take appropriate action depending on whether they develop in a positive or negative direction.

We also looked at factors that are likely to move in a negative rather than positive direction, such as European economic development. For these factors we developed scenario-specific strategy options. For instance, airlines can prepare themselves for weaker economic growth in Europe by increasing the flexibility of their seating arrangements – offering fewer business class seats and more seats in economy during an economic downturn.

We shared our detailed strategic recommendations with experts in the airline industry, who confirmed our findings. The anticipated outcome of the strategy manual is a robust core strategy with specific focal points that can help European network carriers manage the challenges they face. In addition, the strategy manual provides scenario-specific options enabling them to cope with any sudden changes in the factors.

4.6.2
THE SCENARIO COCKPIT

Taking the results generated by the strategy manual, we now applied the scenario cockpit tool. The influence diagram developed for the European airline industry consists of nine influence factors driving the two afore-mentioned uncertainties *degree of regulation of the industry in Europe* and *price sensitivity of the customer base* (Figure 4.32).

We used the influence diagram as a basis for identifying which factors drive the scenarios and for finding indicators for the development of each scenario. We then looked for quantitative or qualitative indicators that could show the development of each factor (Figure 4.33). For influence factors such as *global GDP growth* and *European economic development*, this was easy: We used the GDP figures provided by the International Monetary Fund (for global GDP) and Eurostat (for Europe). For influence factors such as the *political influence of airlines*, finding appropriate indicators was more challenging. Here, we advise airlines to work closely with industry associations such as the International Air Transport Association (IATA) and the Association of European Airlines (AEA) – associations with close ties to regulators that are able to assess such factors.

FIGURE 4.32: INFLUENCE DIAGRAM FOR THE EUROPEAN AIRLINE INDUSTRY

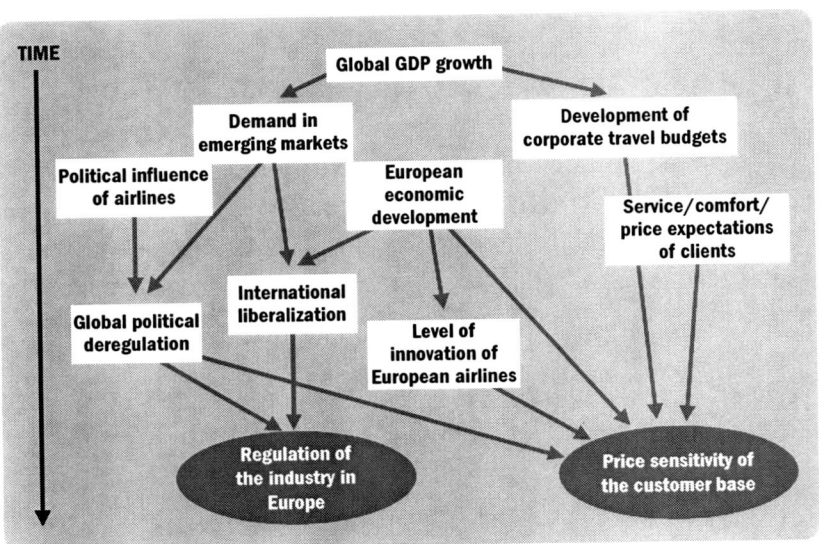

Having drawn up the indicator table, we then defined a value range for each indicator and scenario, allowing us to monitor which scenario actually developed. The scenario study was aimed at the whole industry rather than one specific company, so we defined value ranges for each indicator and scenario broadly. For the first influence factor *development of corporate travel budgets*, for instance, we took the percentage of demand for business versus economy class seats as an indicator. This gave us the indicator range shown in Figure 4.34.

We proceeded in a similar fashion for the remaining indicators. Finally, we transferred the value ranges for the indicators onto an Excel spreadsheet and applied the traffic lights system, to give decision makers in the airline industry a quick indication of which way the world is moving (Figure 4.35).

At the time of the project (summer 2011), the scenario cockpit indicated that the industry was heading in the direction of the scenarios "Network fortress" and

FIGURE 4.33: INDICATOR TABLE FOR THE EUROPEAN AIRLINE INDUSTRY

INFLUENCE FACTORS	INDICATORS
Development of corporate travel budgets	Percentage of demand for business versus economy class seats
Level of innovation of European airlines	Percentage of revenues spent on R&D
Global political deregulation	WTO statistics and tariff data
International liberalization	IATA data on airline market regulation
Global GDP growth	Global GDP data – IMF
Service/comfort/price expectations of clients	Customer surveys
European economic development	European GDP data – Eurostat
Demand in emerging markets	Internal booking data from emerging markets
Political influence of airlines	Political initiatives by airlines under parliamentary review

Critical uncertainty | Trend

FIGURE 4.34: INDICATOR RANGE FOR THE EUROPEAN AIRLINE INDUSTRY (EXAMPLE)

SCENARIOS	PERCENTAGE OF DEMAND FOR BUSINESS VERSUS ECONOMY CLASS SEATS
Network fortress	20% business vs. 80% economy
New horizons	15% business vs. 85% economy
Decline of champions	5% business vs. 95% economy
Europe under siege	10% business vs. 90% economy

FIGURE 4.35: SCENARIO COCKPIT: TRAFFIC LIGHT SYSTEM FOR THE EUROPEAN AIRLINE INDUSTRY

	DEVELOPMENT OF CORPORATE TRAVEL BUDGETS	LEVEL OF INNOVATION OF EUROPEAN AIRLINES	GLOBAL POLITICAL DEREGULATION	INTERNATIONAL LIBERALIZATION
Network fortress	green	yellow	yellow	green
New horizons	red	red	green	red
Decline of champions	red	yellow	red	red
Europe under siege	green	red	yellow	red

"Europe under siege". This told airline managers that their priority should be the strategic actions specifically developed to cope with these two scenarios.

4.7
REFERENCES

Ansoff I. 1975. Managing Strategic Surprise by Response to Weak Signals. *California Management Review* 18(2): 21-33.

Ansoff I. 1965. *Corporate Strategy*. New York: McGraw-Hill.

Ansoff, I., Nakamura G. 2007. *Strategic Management*. Houndmills: Palgrave Macmillan

Bradfield RM., Wright G., Burt G., Cairns G., van der Heijden K. 2005. The Origins and Evolution of Scenario Techniques in long Range Business Planning, *Futures* 37(8): 795-812.

Chermack TJ. 2011. *Scenario Planning in Organizations – How to Create, Use, and Assess Scenarios.* San Francisco: Berrett-Koehler.

De Wit, B., Meyer, R.J.H. 2010. *Strategy Process, Content, Context: an international perspective* 4th ed. London: Cengage Learning, 2010,

Gausemeier J., Plass C., Wenzelmann C. 2009. *Zukunftsorientierte Unternehmensgestaltung: Strategien, Geschäftsprozesse und IT-Systeme für die Produktion von Morgen.* Munich: Hanser.

Hungenberg H. 2010. *Problemlösung und Kommunikation im Management: Vorgehensweisen und Techniken.* Munich: Oldenbourg:

Krampe G. 1985. Ein Früherkennungssystem auf der Basis von Diffusionsfunktionen als Element des strategischen Marketing. In *Strategisches Marketing.* Raffée H., Wiedmann K.-P. (eds.). Stuttgart: Poeschel: 349-369.

Krystek U., Moldenhauer R. 2007. *Handbuch Krisen- und Restrukturierungsmanagement – Generelle Konzepte, Spezialprobleme, Praxisbeispiele.* Stuttgart: Kohlhammer.

Liebl F. 2005. Technologie – Frühaufklärung: Bestandsaufnahme und Perspektiven. *Handbuch Technologie- und Innovationsmanagement: Strategie – Umsetzung – Controlling.* Alber S., Gassmann O. (eds.). Wiesbaden: Gabler: 121-136.

Liebl F. 2002. The Anatomy of Complex Societal Problems and its Implications for OR. *Journal of the Operational Research Society* 53(2): 161-184.

Lindgren M., Bandhold H. 2009. *Scenario Planning – The Link Between Future and Strategy.* Houndmills: Palgrave Macmillan.

Metz B., Davidson OR., Bosch PR., Dave R., Meyer LA. 2007. *Climate Change 2007: Mitigation.* Cambridge, Cambridge University Press.

Mintzberg H. 1994a. *The Rise and Fall of Strategic Planning.* New York: The Free Press.

Mintzberg H. 1994b. The Fall and Rise of Strategic Planning. *Harvard Business Review* 72(1): 107-114.

Schwartz P. 1996. *The Art of the Long View. Planning for the Future in an Uncertain World.* New York: Doubleday Publishing.

van der Heijden K. 2005. *Scenarios: The Art of Strategic Conversation.* Chichester: Wiley.

van der Heijden K., Bradfield R., Burt G., Cairns G., Wright G. 2002: *The Sixth Sense – Accelerating Organizational Learning with Scenarios.* Chichester John Wiley & Sons.

van 't Klooster SA., van Asselt, MBA. 2006. Practicing the scenario-axes technique. *Futures* 38(1): 15-30.

Wack P. 1985a. Scenarios: Uncharted waters ahead. *Harvard Business Review* 63(5): 73-89.

Wack P. 1985b. Scenarios: Shooting the Rapids. *Harvard Business Review* 63(6): 139-150.

Welsch C. 2010. *Organisationale Trägheit und ihre Wirkung auf die strategische Früherkennung von Unternehmenskrisen.* Wiesbaden: Gabler.

Wright G., Cairns G. 2011. *Scenario Thinking: Practical Approaches to the Future.* Houndmills: Palgrave MacMillan.

Wilson, I. 2006. *Scenario Planning Handbook: Developing Strategies in Uncertain Times.* Mason: Thomson South Western

Wulf, T., Stubner, S., Meißner, P., Brands, C. 2012. Szenariobasierte strategische Planung in volatilen Umfeldern. *Zeitschrift für Controlling und Management* special issue 2/2012: 34-38.

Wulf T., Meißner P., Stubner S. 2010. *A Scenario-based Approach to Strategic Planning – Integrating Planning and Process Perspectives of Strategy.* Leipzig: HHL Working Paper.

5.
Scenario-based strategic planning
Using scenario planning to identify opportunities in a multi-sector industry
NICKLAS HOLGERSSON, DUCE GOTORA

SCENARIO-BASED STRATEGIC PLANNING

In 2011, Roland Berger Strategy Consultants conducted a scenario planning project for one of the world's largest companies. The company in question has significant market positions in several sectors and is known for its innovative technology, diverse product range and high service standards. As a part of an ongoing initiative to define future business concepts, the company hired Roland Berger to provide an outside-in, out-of-the-box perspective of trends and to develop 2020 scenarios applicable to a range of customer sectors within the manufacturing industry. This also included identifying business opportunities through innovative "ideation workshops" with cross-functional company representatives and external experts in Europe, North America and Asia. Roland Berger also supported the development of detailed business cases for selected opportunities and ensured an effective hand-over in order to promote the build-up of organisational capabilities for long-term innovation.

5.1 INTRODUCTION

The manufacturing industry comprises the processing and manufacturing of items and came into being with the occurrence of technological and socio-economic transformations in the Western world in the eighteenth century. With each progressive era since, manufacturing has become more globalized and increasingly complex. Today, the manufacturing industry accounts for a significant share of the industrial sector in developed countries and is growing rapidly in emerging economies such as the BRIC and VISTA countries (VISTA countries: Vietnam, Indonesia, South Africa, Turkey, Argentina.). The manufacturing industry is important for an economy as it employs a significant share of the labor force and produces materials required by sectors of strategic importance, such as national infrastructure and defence. According to some economists, manufacturing is a wealth-producing sector of an economy, whereas the service sector tends to be wealth-consuming. In the US and France manufacturing as a share of the economy has been on the decline for many years now. Experts there are discussing reindustrialization as a way to strengthen the national economy. How the manufacturing industry could develop in the future is of great importance not only to governments but also to participating companies and those supplying into the industry.

5.2
CHALLENGE AND OBJECTIVES

The manufacturing industry covers a wide range of sectors, from raw material extraction such as mining and chemicals to raw material primary processing such as metals manufacturing and materials fabrication in the automotive and aerospace sectors. The manufacturing industry also includes high tech sectors such as electronics and telecommunications and lower tech sectors such as textile and food & beverage. The size of players in the manufacturing industry ranges from small SMEs to large multinational corporations. A lot of "hidden champions" are industrial manufacturers. All in all, the manufacturing industry is made up of a variety of sectors with different drivers, customers and characteristics. This makes it challenging to develop coherent scenarios for the manufacturing industry as a whole. Despite this challenge, Roland Berger Strategy Consultants recently took up the challenge to define a set of scenarios and appropriate business opportunities within the general manufacturing industry. The concept development was grounded in the customer and industry needs and trends of 2020 and factored in input from internal client stakeholders and external experts.

5.3
METHODOLOGY/APPROACH

Our scenario planning approach is based on the methodology jointly developed by Roland Berger and HHL. In our project we have gone through five process steps that are based on four of the six steps of the HHL-Roland Berger approach to scenario-based strategic planning. However, due to the goal of the project, which focussed on the identification of business opportunities and business cases rather than a traditional strategy development, we slightly modified the original approach in the strategy definition phase and neglected the monitoring process of the overall approach. Thus, we were able to utilize the advantages of the methodology and the dedicated tools to help our client plan for multiple options in the challenging and volatile business environment they faced. Also, the approach allowed managers to integrate and align internal and external perspectives to challenge existing assumptions and mind-sets.

FIGURE 5.1: THE FIVE STEPS OF THE SCENARIO PROCESS

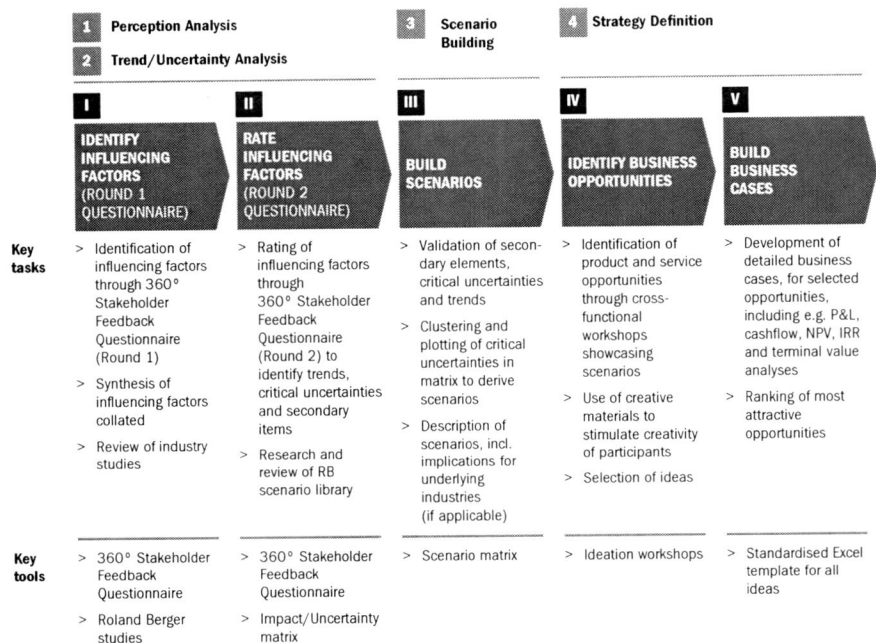

5.3.1
IDENTIFYING AND RATING INFLUENCING FACTORS

In order to analyse the influencing factors of the global manufacturing industry, we used the Roland Berger 360° Stakeholder Feedback Questionnaire. Influencing factors across STEEP (Social, Technological, Economic, Environmental and Political/Legal) dimensions were identified in the first round. The questionnaire was submitted to internal stakeholders (across functions) and external experts (e.g. from industry, think tanks, academia, etc.) across key manufacturing sectors and geographies. Respondents identified 90 mutually exclusive influencing factors – of these, 25% were political/legal factors. These factors were then clustered and sent out in the second round which focused on the rating of each influencing factor against two key criteria:

FIGURE 5.2: TRENDS, CRITICAL UNCERTAINTIES AND SECONDARY ELEMENTS WITHIN THE IMPACT-UNCERTAINTY GRID

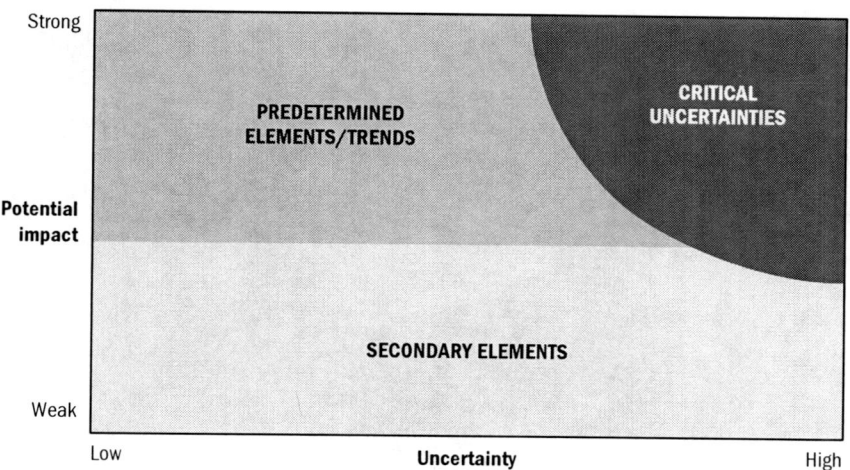

♦ Impact – How significant will the impact of the influencing factor be in the global context?

♦ Uncertainty – What is the degree of uncertainty that the influencing factor will indeed occur?

Using the ratings, influencing factors were categorized into trends (low uncertainty, high impact), critical uncertainties (high uncertainty but high impact) and secondary elements (low impact):

Examples of trends identified:
♦ Growth of developing countries as end-use markets (e.g. China and India)
♦ Growth of next wave of low cost manufacturing bases (e.g. VISTA countries)
♦ Ageing population in developed countries
♦ Use of nanotechnology, miniaturization and micro-electronics
♦ Transition to light-weight materials (e.g. composites)

FIGURE 5.3: CLUSTERING OF UNCERTAINTIES AND BUILDING OF SCENARIOS

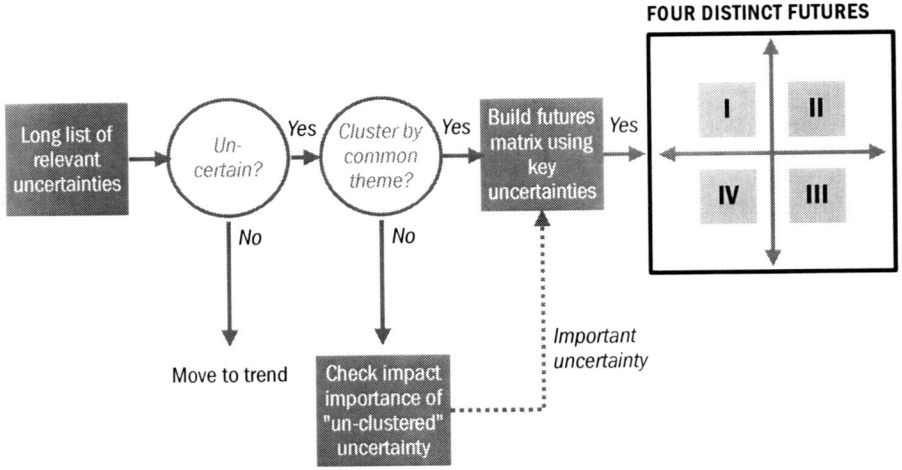

5.3.2
BUILDING SCENARIOS

Four distinct scenarios were developed for the industrial sector after eliminating the secondary elements, validating trends and clustering key uncertainties: The process used in this case was a slightly modified version of our original approach.

Protectionism and Resource Intensity were determined to be the key uncertainties that would have the most impact on the industrial sector as a whole. Hence, these two dimensions were chosen as the axes of the scenario matrix.

SCENARIO DIMENSION: PROTECTIONISM
Protectionism refers to the mechanism by which nations and regions limit trade to preserve and enhance their own interests and agenda. This is often played out in

the context of preserving critical raw materials by imposing duties and tariffs, and foreign ownership restrictions. Protectionism can significantly impact the landscape of intellectual property, patent adherence and industrial espionage.

Impact of the Protectionism Dimension
The Protectionism dimension impacts the footprint and degree of production and logistics complexity, with large manufacturing clusters seeking economies of scale on the one hand and localized small-scale production and limited cross-regional trade on the other.

SCENARIO DIMENSION: RESOURCE INTENSITY
Resource Intensity refers to degree of usage and impact on/of natural resources such as metals, water, air and climate. Government subsidies and regulations can play a key role in determining the resource intensity of the industrial economy, as can consumer preferences for green and sustainable products.

Impact of the Resource Intensity Dimension
The Resource Intensity dimension has considerable implications for product development, production processes, and end-product handling, with the growth of alternative materials and production technologies easing the resource constraints in one extreme, while continued scale manufacturing with current technologies and power sources continues unabated in the other.

The following sections outline these dimensions further and describe each of the four plausible scenarios that are based on these key uncertainties.

5.3.3
FOUR SCENARIOS FOR GLOBAL MANUFACTURING INDUSTRY

The developed scenarios apply to the global manufacturing sector. This comprises nine different industries: Energy, Mining, Cement, Chemicals, Metal Manufacturing, Fabricated Metal Goods, Machine Manufacturing, Automotive, and Aerospace.

While the scenarios developed broadly apply to all the above mentioned industries, they differ by industry in the degree to which each plays out. The industry-specific nuances were described within detailed narratives for each scenario.

The four scenarios described below are extreme, and while the world may never reach one of these extremes, it could start tracking towards them:

Antagonistic Age: *describes a future characterized by protectionism (on city, country and regional level) and the existence of trade blocs. However, governments advocate sustainability standards. Companies are forced to engage in frugal innovation for regional markets.*

Resource Intensity – Environmental standards have been set by national governments within trade blocs and are accepted by corporations and civil society. However, as standards have been set to primarily suit countries within the respective trade blocs, there is no level playing field across regions. Furthermore, natural resources such as water are scarce in many regions due to geographical constraints. In some countries, several sources of natural resources have even been nationalized.

Protectionism – Protectionist policies have adversely affected export opportunities, thereby limiting the global addressable market for businesses. Trade bloc formation has largely been driven by access to complementary resources allowing for self-sustainability of trade blocs. This has led to the formation of many unholy alliances and to significant differences in growth between regions. Restricted trade flows have also led to increased extraction of raw materials in difficult locations and the development of substitute materials.

Consumers – Given restrictions in global trade and natural resource scarcity in many countries, consumers have come to terms with less product choice. As global brands and products are less prevalent, consumers are satisfied with products that are "good enough" as long as they are customized to regional tastes and requirements. Strict environmental regulations play a key role in dictating the types of products available in the market.

Business – Regional companies, with small-scale plants serving domestic markets, dominate. Given the restricted trade flows, many companies have been forced to integrate vertically. However, many manufacturers struggle to achieve economies of scale given smaller addressable markets. Due to the high cost of scarce raw materials, companies have adopted initiatives to turn scrap and waste into usable input for production processes. Furthermore, they have invested in the development of new materials (such as composites, ceramics and bio materials) and developed new processes to improve productivity. While there has been growth in open innovation between trade bloc partners, limited knowledge-exchange between trade blocs has led to the development of numerous different standards in many areas.

WINNERS & LOSERS

Nations with abundant natural resources thrive until resource poor countries develop innovations. Those with raw materials will focus on production technologies, while those without will focus on design or the development of alternative materials. These new materials are designed for specific applications, and a new periodic table is created for nano-materials. Winning regions include Western Europe, North America, China, India, Brazil, and Australia – these either are self-sufficient or have valuable expertise and skills to trade for commodities they do not have. The Middle East and Japan lose in this scenario, while China and the US are well placed due to their military might. Industries that win include Energy, especially renewables, due to the high uptake of renewable energy benefitting providers and equipment manufacturers, micro generation and co-generation technologies. The automotive industry sees growth through electric cars. However, cars are no longer global and the use of gas guzzlers is further restricted. Companies unable to adapt to this new reality do not survive. Cement and Energy industries are hit hard by the need to lower resource intensity, as is the Aerospace industry due to the decrease in large commercial aircraft.

Key Success Factors in this future
- Compliance with regional environmental standards to satisfy regulations
- Access to natural resources (or cooperation with organizations for indirect access)
- In resource-scarce countries, retention and attraction of human capital to develop substitute materials

- Restructured operations (incl. small-scale plants) to supply local/regional markets

Polarized World: *describes a future in which globalization has been restrained by the prioritization of national interests. Given protectionist policies and lack of common regulatory enforcement, there are widely different economic and political agendas.*

Resource Intensity – Basic environmental standards have been set by national governments, but are not consistently enforced – a blind eye is often turned to emissions. Furthermore, the increased discharge of effluent has worsened water pollution. In many countries, eco-systems have been severely damaged due to excessively aggressive excavation techniques. Replacement of fossil fuels has only been partial. International bodies have failed to coordinate the diverse interests of countries.

Protectionism – Given the prevalence of tariffs and quotas, there are vast differences in access to resources across countries. As resource-rich countries have resorted to strict protectionist policies, there are economic disparities and geopolitical imbalances. The world is divided into two groups: the "haves" and the "have-nots". As a result, there are frequent protests and incidents of social upheaval.

Consumers – Given the limited enforcement of green standards, there is limited environmental awareness in society. There is increased consumerism with preference for disposable low-end and mid-range products, tailored to regional requirements. In surveys on consumer attitudes, Generation Y respondents show only secondary concern for the impact of their consumption on the environment.

Business – Multinational companies have had to restructure and reduce their manufacturing footprint to primarily serve regional markets. Many large OEMs have gone bankrupt as they have been too slow to reduce their high fixed costs. International oil companies (IOCs) have been replaced by national powerhouses. The main driver for the development of alternative materials has been the shortage of raw materials rather than the desire to comply with environmental standards. For companies based in countries with raw material shortages, it has become vital to attract human capital which improves companies' competitiveness through innovation (e.g. development of substitute materials). National companies with new innovations are careful not to leak out their trade secrets.

WINNERS & LOSERS
Nationalized companies in resource rich countries grow at the expense of large multinationals, resulting in an economic power shift that leaves resource poor countries like Japan in ruins. Countries with natural resources focus on production technologies, while resource poor countries focus on the design and development of alternative materials. Resource rich regions, as well as large markets and technologically advanced nations prosper. These include North America, China, India, Russia, Brazil, Australia, and the Middle East. Japan and Western Europe lose out in this future. Steel and cement use grows in developing regions with ambitious agendas to catch up in terms of infrastructure, and a lot of chemical manufacturing shifts to China, Russia, and the Middle East to be closer to end use markets. The Energy sector continues to be important, with fossil fuels dominating. The Mining sector focuses on underground mining trying to reach hard to get minerals. The Automotive sector is impacted by fragmented markets – there are no global cars like the Ford Focus. Aerospace is impacted due to the decrease in new fuel efficient large commercial aircraft. Japan and Western Europe lose in this future, while North America, China, India, Russia, Brazil, Australia, and the Middle East are the winners.

Key Success Factors in this future
- Access to natural resources (or cooperation with organizations for indirect access)
- Focus on cost optimization through cost effective exploitation of resources to ensure competitively priced products
- Restructured operations (incl. small-scale plants) to supply local/regional markets

Squandering Society: *describes a future in which international bodies such as the WTO have promoted and facilitated free trade. However, there is limited willingness among countries to address environmental matters.*

Resource Intensity – Self-compliance on basic environmental standards is the main instrument to stimulate sustainability practices. Several countries have not yet ratified the Kyoto Protocol as it is widely believed that such agreements lead to lost competitiveness in the global marketplace. Fossil fuels are still widely used as there has been a low uptake of renewable energy following the withdrawal of government subsidies.

Protectionism – The free market has been deemed the most effective way to allocate resources. There are neither regional boundaries nor significant impediments to the mobility of people and goods. While increased globalization has resulted in a more integrated world economy, it has also led to "brain drain" in certain countries as skilled professionals have pursued opportunities elsewhere. Furthermore, poor regions have been further exploited as businesses look for cost advantages.

Consumers – Consumers pursue personal utility and pay little attention to the environmental impact of their consumption. They demand cheap products and put little emphasis on sustainability. Given low trade barriers, consumers have grown accustomed to the availability of global products and brands. Fierce competition among companies on a global level is regarded as necessary in order to ensure that products become cheaper, faster and better.

Business – The interests of multinational companies shape international trade and discourse. The manufacturing environment is characterized by intense competition for scarce raw materials, global mass production and high supply chain complexity. The adoption of alternative materials is purely driven by market economics (e.g. through improved functionality and performance). Similarly, sustainability initiatives, such as waste reduction, are only pursued if they result in productivity gains and lower costs. Given production on a global scale, late customization proliferates. To enable and coordinate interactions between a range of players in the business arena, Google has emerged as the new power broker.

WINNERS & LOSERS
Winners include nations with the capacity to produce goods on a mass-scale at a low cost. With giant and complex supply chains, the ability to orchestrate supply chains and delay customization creates immense business value – technology companies that can form the glue that holds the manufacturing economy together

increasingly capture value. Large-scale fossil fuel based power plants dominate the energy sector, resulting in open pit mining for coal and increased exploitation for resources in Africa. Gas guzzlers dominate the automotive landscape, with millions for first time car buyers in the emerging markets of China and India craving prestige cars from the West. Winning regions include North America, China, India, Russia, Vietnam, and Indonesia. Renewable energy takes a backseat as does micro-generation technology. The electric vehicle technology is relegated to a niche. Western Europe and Japan lose in this future.

Key Success Factors in this future
- Access to raw materials
- Development of new materials to primarily deliver functionality and improved performance
- Focus on cost optimization to enable competitively priced products
- Mass production capabilities to address global demand
- Global supply chain
- Mass marketing
- Global brand

Green Capitalism: *describes a future in which public and private sectors worldwide take social, economic and environmental aspects of sustainability into account. A global governance model promoting sustainability is in place.*

Resource Intensity – Adherence to a comprehensive range of sustainability standards has been achieved through stakeholder participation and cooperation between national governments. Furthermore, industry is a committed partner, collaborating with government and civil society to achieve zero waste objectives. Recycling of waste (e.g. used oils and lubricants) and water has become a cornerstone of society. Renewable energy accounts for the majority of energy supply.

Protectionism – Markets are characterized by low levels of protectionism. The lack of regional boundaries is seen as an opportunity for the free movement of people and ideas. Across countries, there is a collective emphasis on the joint identification of new business models to harness knowledge, insights and skills. Resource-rich countries collaborate with disadvantaged countries to ensure build-up of infrastructure which enable widespread use of green energy.

Consumers – Consumers demand products from across the world, as long as the product lifecycle is green. Given the importance of traceability, most companies producing environmentally unfriendly products have been denounced by consumer groups keeping a watchful eye on corporate players through social media. On the local level, there is increased influence of local community groups promoting green issues. Green innovation is recognized and rewarded.

Business – Many previously vertically integrated companies have disintegrated to specialize in niche green technologies. Many corporations also work closely with the public sector in R&D. However, there are frequent lawsuits for IP infringements as IP has become the key differentiator in an innovation-focused world. Manufacturing processes requiring less energy and water have been developed in order to promote fulfilment of strict environmental objectives. There has also been a rapid uptake of new materials and modular made-to-order production methods. The significant use of sensors in products and processes has also enabled greener manufacturing. For producers, competition for renewable feedstock is fierce as they compete with food industry companies which have significant buying power.

WINNERS & LOSERS

There is a high uptake in renewable energy benefitting providers and equipment manufacturers alike. Micro-generation technologies are widespread, as are electric vehicles with the required infrastructure in place. Designers are the winners in this future and small "cottage design / manufacturers" are able to compete with large manufacturers as design is decoupled with traditional manufacturing. New materials are designed for specific applications and environments. Additive manufacturing clearly takes a hold. There is increased use of steel and glass, especially in construction processes that also lowers the demand for cement. Regional winners include Western Europe, North America, China, India, Japan, and Brazil. The traditional fossil fuels dominated economies of the Middle East are losers in this scenario. This future also sees a lower need for energy reducing fossil fuel based power generation; this also impacts the mining industry negatively as substitute materials grow and consumers also actively lobby against excessive mining of resources. The Middle East is a loser in this future.

Key Success Factors in this future
- Compliance with environmental standards to satisfy regulations and consumer requirements
- Development of light-weight materials and biodegradable components
- Development of green product life cycle including a green global supply chain
- Adoption of modular manufacturing philosophy with made-to-order production
- Protection of IPs
- Mass marketing

5.3.4
IDENTIFYING OPPORTUNITIES AND BUILDING BUSINESS CASES

In order to account for the goal of the scenario project, we focussed on the identification of new business opportunities and business cases rather than the development of robust strategies in the last step of the process.

The scenarios developed were communicated in an 'ideation workshop' to a cross-functional group including client teams from Strategy, M&A, Marketing, Operations and Engineering departments. Engaged through presentations, role play and group work, ideas pertaining to the distinct scenarios were generated. Facilitated by consultants, the ideation workshop also had business illustrators to visually capture ideas that were hard to describe with written word only. Participants were encouraged to generate ideas covering all possible products and/or services – these were classified as being core, adjacent, stretch or blue sky.

During the two day long workshop, robust ideas were grouped by theme and refined. The final step was the prioritization of ideas based on the agreed criteria below:
- Product/service characteristics
- Potential market size

FIGURE 5.4: SPECTRUM OF POSSIBLE IDEAS DEPENDING ON TIME FRAME AND DIVERGENCE FROM CORE BUSINESS

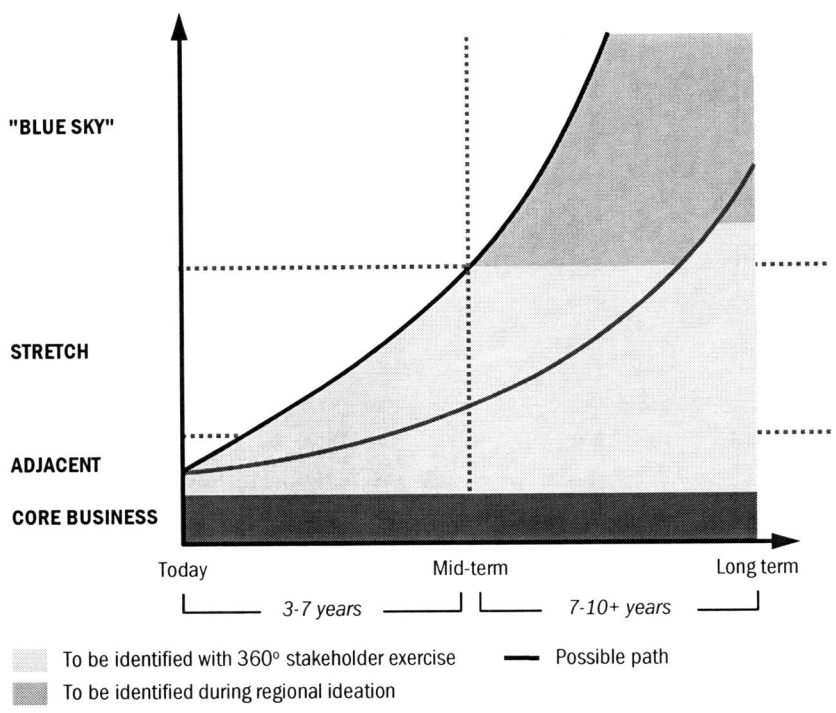

- Untapped market need
- Potential customers
- Client's right to play

After the two day ideation workshop, detailed business cases were created for each priority business opportunity. These opportunities were ranked using e.g. NPV and IRR metrics in order to inform the decision-making process of which opportunity to pursue in each potential scenario.

5.4
BEST PRACTICES

During the course of the project, several best practices were followed.

In the early stages, it proved of utmost importance to leverage the network of Roland Berger experts from different geographies and sectors. By combining their input with that of external experts, we identified a collectively exhaustive and mutually exclusive list of influencing factors and achieved high response rates. As the questionnaires were distributed around the holiday season, it was crucial to allow for sufficient time for responses. Clear questionnaire instructions, structure and content ensured that experts easily could understand the objective of the exercise and complete their sector-specific part.

Once influencing factors had been classified into trends, critical uncertainties and secondary elements, access to up-to-date market studies and data was vital in order to challenge and validate the classification of influencing factors. For this validation the complementary use of Roland Berger and client data is key, while the early sharing of arising insights will achieve client buy in.

During the scenario building process, workshops with the client are required to agree on scenario content and names. Narratives must cover all aspects which may be of interest to the client, including the impact on the underlying sectors. Furthermore, any schematics used must frame the scenario content is a clear manner.

In order to identify business opportunities within scenarios, a cross-functional client team must be secured for the "ideation workshops". Such a team could include representatives from e.g. Strategy, M&A, Marketing, Operations and R&D. A range of supporting materials – including posters, videos and objects – should be used to bring scenarios to life during the workshops. Exercises such as role play can also add value. Pre-reads can be used in order to stimulate the creativity of participants. It is important to moderate the workshops and ensure that the discussion is kept at a strategic level. Otherwise, participants will tend to focus on functional constraints which will inhibit the identification of opportunities in the 2020 context.

5.5 CONCLUSIONS

Trying to identify business opportunities in an uncertain future, for multi-sector industries characterized by a kaleidoscope of possibilities, is a tough challenge.

Each of the scenarios identified represents an extreme vision of the future. While the world may never reach one of these extremes, it is likely to be shaped by elements from the different scenarios. In a given region, industries could exhibit characteristics from the different scenarios given industry-specific dynamics impacting the degree of protectionism and resource intensity. For instance, elements from Antagonistic Age could characterize the automotive industry while elements from Green Capitalism could characterize the Aerospace industry. Hence, in the future, several elements from the extreme scenarios are likely to come into play on a regional basis. Companies that will succeed are those who look for opportunities that cut across the variety of futures with very little "tweaking" in order to capture the full potential of any one of the possible scenarios.

6.
The benefits of scenario-based planning
How scenario-based strategic planning affects the behavior of managers

PHILIP MEISSNER

SCENARIO-BASED STRATEGIC PLANNING

Scenario-based strategic planning provides a strategy framework that enables managers to better manage the uncertain environmental conditions that many industries face today. The method's greatest potential lies in the fact that it provides flexible rather than unidimensional strategies and thus potentially improves the quality of decisions in companies. However, previous research has only analyzed the impact of scenario planning implicitly. We therefore present a concept that describes how scenario-based strategic planning can be used to increase decision quality. To this end, we focus on the three key drivers of decision quality as identified and described in previous research: decisions should be comprehensive, fast and unbiased. In this chapter, we analyze these factors in depth and suggest what is necessary to achieve them in a strategic decision-making process. Furthermore, we show that scenario-based strategic planning provides a methodological foundation for implementing such a process in corporate practice as it combines quick application, which increases the speed of decision making, with open strategic thinking, which reduces bias and increases the comprehensiveness of decisions.

6.1 INTRODUCTION

In the previous chapters, we described the HHL/Roland Berger approach to scenario-based strategic planning and showed how it can be applied. We now turn to the advantages of the method. Specifically, in this chapter we show how scenario-based strategic planning can be used to increase the quality of decisions and to develop more flexible strategies in corporate practice.

Strategic decision making is one of the most important tasks of strategic management. However, in recent years it has become more difficult for corporate managers due to an increasingly volatile, uncertain and complex environment (Chermack, 2011). This is reflected in the quality of strategic decisions made in corporate practice, which is often insufficient. For example, for many years Austrian Airlines neglected the threat of low-cost carriers such as Ryanair and EasyJet. When the company finally woke up to the competition, it was almost too late. It was forced to react with major cost cuts and restructuring programs (Wulf et al., 2011).

Media-Saturn also underestimated the growth of new sales channels such as online shopping. This gave one of its largest competitors, Amazon, time to establish itself as the leader in the online market in almost every segment including consumer electronics.

Companies such as United Parcel Service (UPS) have shown that the quality of strategic decisions can be increased by a good strategy process. UPS implemented a comprehensive strategic planning process at the beginning of the 1990s, which prepared them for the forthcoming strategic challenges and aligned the organization (Garvin and Levesque, 2006). However, the majority of strategic decisions in companies still show room for improvement today. Lovallo and Sibony (2010) found that only 28% of executives were satisfied with the decision quality achieved in their strategy processes (Lovallo/Sibony, 2010). Bad strategic decisions can lead to significant costs for corporations (Milkman et al., 2009). For example, a recent study found that ineffective decision making can decrease total shareholder return by nearly six percentage points (Blenko et al., 2010).

The significant impact of strategic decision making on performance has inspired a large body of research analyzing the underlying drivers of decision quality (Amason, 1996; Priem et al., 1996; Wally/Baum, 1994). The majority of this research focuses on comprehensiveness (Miller, 2008) and speed (Forbes, 2005), two important characteristics of the strategy process influencing decision effectiveness and corporate performance (Eisenhardt, 1989). The studies find support for the hypotheses that comprehensiveness and speed make a positive contribution to firm performance in dynamic environments (Judge/Miller, 1991; Walters/Bhuian 2004) that change both frequently and unpredictably (Hart/Banbury, 1994). They thus provide a strong indication of how the strategic decision-making process should be designed in today's uncertain business environment.

However, the behavioral aspects of decision quality have attracted little attention in the strategic management literature. Behavioral decision theory focuses on the analysis of cognitive biases, which have been shown to reduce decision quality (Milkman et al., 2009; Das/Teng, 1999). These biases are systematic deviations from economic rationality (Kahneman/Tversky, 2000), which limit rational judgment in decision-making processes (Bazerman/Moore, 2009). Reducing biases and increasing the resulting decision quality in the strategy process has been shown to increase return on investment by seven percentage points in a recent study (Lovallo et al., 2011). We therefore consider it important to address the influence of cognitive biases and their effect on decision quality to ensure a more holistic understanding of the driving forces behind decision quality and corporate performance (Lovallo/Sibony, 2010).

The literature also largely neglects the influence of scenario-based strategic planning on decision quality. This is surprising, as the research has identified many advantages to this method, particularly in environments and industries that face a high level of uncertainty (van der Heijden, 2005; Schoemaker, 1995). The main advantages are that the method considers both internal and external stakeholder perspectives, and it challenges assumptions and mindsets. It thus enables decision makers to broaden their perception of possible changes in their environment (Wack, 1985a; Wack, 1985b; Schoemaker, 1993; Schoemaker, 1995; Healey/Hodgkinson, 2008). At the same time, scenario planning integrates uncertainty into the strategy process and increases flexibility by planning for multiple contingencies (van der Heijden, 2005).

These benefits can be summarized as two main effects. First, by broadening management's perception and integrating outside experts into the strategy process (Schoemaker, 1995), scenario planning can increase the quality of strategic decisions. Second, scenario planning leads to more flexible and adaptable strategies, which improve the company's responsiveness to changes in its environment. In particular, the potential to enhance the quality of decisions and consequently boost corporate performance provides companies with a significant lever for improving strategic management (Dean/Sharfman, 1996).

This chapter bridges the gap between scenario planning and decision quality. It integrates two streams of research, one focused on decision comprehensiveness and speed, and the other on behavioral decision making. It also shows how decision quality can be improved by implementing a quick, comprehensive and unbiased strategic decision-making process. Further, it reveals how scenario-based strategic planning provides a methodological foundation for implementing this process in practice.

6.2 DECISION-MAKING COMPREHENSIVENESS AND SPEED

It is widely accepted that the quality of strategic decisions significantly contributes to the performance of companies (Eisenhardt, 1989). The majority of studies analyzing this relationship focus on two specific characteristics of the decision-making process, namely comprehensiveness and speed. We examine these characteristics below.

6.2.1 DECISION MAKING COMPREHENSIVENESS

In 2010, Lufthansa performed a holistic analysis of the airline market based on a scenario-planning process. The results of this process illustrate the positive effects of comprehensive decision making and strategic planning. Most importantly, the comprehensive external analysis conducted enabled management to identify key forces driving the industry in the short and medium term. Thanks to this process, the company spotted a shift in both demand and competition toward Asia and the Middle East. They could reflect this development in their strategy and were able to respond proactively to changes in their environment (Wulf et al., 2011).

The concept of "decision-making comprehensiveness" is widely described in the literature. "Decision-making comprehensiveness" is the extent to which a corporation's management applies an extensive process when facing new challenges or opportunities (Miller, 2008; Dean/Sharfman, 1996). While early research on decision quality suggested that organizations should implement lean processes to reduce information overload (Braybrooke/Lindblom, 1963), more recent studies support the use of comprehensive processes, as such processes enhance rational decision making in corporate practice (for a review, see Miller, 2008). The research shows that comprehensive decision making allows decision makers to be more realistic in their evaluation of the company's environment, which should improve both decision quality and performance (Fredrickson, 1984; Atuahene-Gima/Li, 2004).

However, the dynamism of the company's environment is crucial for determining the right level of analytical rigor or comprehensiveness in the decision-making process (Hough/White, 2003). For this reason, past research debated the question of whether comprehensive approaches were more beneficial for turbulent or for stable environments. On the one hand, a comprehensive approach is regarded as beneficial in turbulent environments as more information is needed in order for a company to be able to adapt in an environment that is changing quickly (Miller, 2008). On the other hand, a comprehensive approach may be appropriate in stable environments as in such situations comprehensiveness can be easily safeguarded: there are fewer time constraints, so the company can carefully consider alternatives, and important developments take place less quickly (Glick et al., 1993).

This debate is reflected in empirical studies on decision comprehensiveness. Such studies have yielded mixed results with regard to the influence of specific environmental characteristics. Fredrickson (1984) finds that comprehensiveness has positive effects on performance in stable industries (Fredrickson, 1984), while in unstable or turbulent industries its influence is negative (Fredrickson/Mitchell, 1984). Other studies find to the contrary (Eisenhardt, 1989; Glick et al., 1993).

A recent study by Miller (2008) appears to resolve this conflict. Miller shows that the relationship between comprehensiveness and performance follows an inverted U-shape in stable industries. In other words, comprehensiveness boosts performance to a certain degree and then, after this point, works against it due to the higher levels of complexity. In turbulent and uncertain environmental conditions, in which change is unpredictable, Miller finds that comprehensiveness has a positive effect on performance, a finding that agrees with the vast majority of previous studies (Miller, 2008).

Past empirical studies focus on performance and neglect the direct impact of comprehensiveness on decision quality (Forbes, 2007). However, we may assume that a direct connection exists between the two: comprehensiveness increases performance by improving decision quality. Empirical studies from the last decade indicate that companies should implement a moderately comprehensive decision-making process in stable environments and a highly comprehensive process in turbulent environments. Given the growing uncertainty of today's economic world, we can assume that few industries are truly stable and that comprehensiveness is indeed a core characteristic of effective decision-making processes.

Previous research finds that, to be fully comprehensive, a decision-making process should have two key characteristics:
1. It should include a wide range of alternatives (Fredrickson, 1984)
2. It should include high levels of investigatory activities (Miller, 2008), such as environmental scanning and an open search for new information (Atuahene-Gima/Li, 2004)

Companies that ensure that their decision-making process includes these two characteristics should enjoy better decision quality and performance.

6.2.2
DECISION SPEED

The second important characteristic of decision-making processes is "decision speed". "Decision speed" is the time it takes an organization to conduct the decision-making process, from the initial discussion of alternatives to the final commitment (Forbes, 2005; Eisenhardt, 1989). To give an extreme, negative example: When Lufthansa launched Germanwings in 2002 to compete in the low-cost market, Ryanair had already been active in this segment for more than ten years.

Empirical studies show that fast decision-making processes increase performance in dynamic environments (Eisenhardt, 1989; Judge/Miller, 1991) and under different environmental conditions (Baum/Wally, 2003). This is due to the fact that important opportunities such as launching new products or exploiting efficiency gains can be realized more quickly (Stevenson/Gumpert, 1985; Baum/Wally, 2003).

However, decision speed does not imply rushed decision making. Studies identify average speeds of 4.6 months (Forbes, 2005), 7.7 months (Eisenhardt, 1989) and 18.7 months (Judge/Miller, 1991). Furthermore, there is no contradiction between a high level of comprehensiveness and speed. In fact, quick decision making only yields good results if comprehensive analysis is not sacrificed to speed (Kahneman et al., 1982). Eisenhardt (1989) finds that the speed of the decision-making process can be increased by considering various alternatives at the same time, which benefits both comprehensiveness and speed. A study by Wally and Baum finds that a low level of formalization also contributes to decision speed. This underscores the fact that the quality of the decision-making process does not depend on a high level of structural formalization but rather on the simultaneous consideration of different alternatives (Wally/Baum, 1994).

Thus, two things are necessary for a decision-making process to be fast, decisions to be of good quality and company performance to benefit:
1. Simultaneous consideration of multiple alternatives (Fredrickson, 1984)
2. A low degree of formalization (Wally/Baum, 1994)

In summary, the decision-making process is crucial in achieving high-quality decisions and boosting a company's performance. The comprehensiveness and speed of the decision-making process are particularly important, improving the quality of the company's decisions and its performance in today's increasingly turbulent environment.

6.3 COGNITIVE BIASES

Existing management research largely ignores the behavioral aspects of the decision-making process. Below, we discuss the importance of this area and analyze its effect on the quality of decisions.

Media-Saturn, whose main brands are Media Markt and Saturn, has gained much of its competitive advantage from positioning itself as the price leader in the electronics retail industry. It is well-known for its groundbreaking advertising campaigns with slogans such as "Geiz ist geil" ("greed is great") and "Saubillig und noch viel mehr" ("dirt cheap and much more besides"). Today, however, the company faces severe pressure from online competition. It has not yet found a strategy for using its strong brands in the online market, despite considerable efforts. This lack of investment in the online market may in part be the result of the management's confidence (or overconfidence) in their competitive position in the bricks-and-mortar retail market. A similar mindset is found in many companies today. It has a key influence on strategic decisions and can often lead to bad decisions.

Although neglected in management research, the behavioral aspects of decision making in general have been widely analyzed in studies in other areas in recent decades. Research in this area began in the 1970s with the groundbreaking work of Tversky and Kahneman (1974; 1981). Their findings have been continuously added to and refined over the years. Research into behavioral decision making looks primarily at cognitive biases, i.e. deviations from traditional economic rationality (Kahneman/Tversky, 2000). Such biases have been found to decrease the quality of decisions (Milkman et al., 2009).

Biases are caused by the heuristics that decision makers use to evaluate information (Bazerman/Moore, 2009). Recent research reevaluates the role of heuristics in the decision-making process. Long regarded as entirely negative, new findings suggest that they can in fact improve decisions under specific environmental conditions (Kahneman/Klein, 2009; Dane/Pratt, 2007). Specifically, if heuristics are used for intuitive decision making based on previous experience, they may lead to quicker and more effective business decisions (Hodgkinson et al., 2009).

Whether heuristics are advantageous or disadvantageous for decision making depends very much on the predictability of the environment. Here, Kahneman and Klein (2009) differentiate between high-validity and low-validity environments. In high-validity environments, relationships between events can be objectively and easily identified, while in low-validity environments, outcomes are largely unpredictable. The authors conclude that intuitive judgments based on individual expertise can be trusted in high-validity environments, whereas in low-validity environments intuition based on heuristics likely leads to biases (Kahneman/Klein, 2009).

These findings agree with research in the field of behavioral strategy. The research suggests that biases occur particularly often in strategic decisions where managers are faced with a high level of environmental uncertainty (Hodgkinson et al., 1999), creating low-validity decision environments (Kahneman/Klein, 2009; Kahneman/Klein, 2010). So it is particularly important to analyze the impact of biases and potential strategies to counteract them in strategic decision environments in business (Kahneman et al., 2011; Lovallo/Sibony, 2010).

Researchers have identified and analyzed a large number of different biases (Kahneman/Tversky, 2000). They occur for decision makers irrespective of their experience or education (Bateman/Zeithaml, 1989a; Bateman/Zeithaml, 1989b). Two such biases are of particular importance in the strategy process: "overconfidence bias" and "framing bias" (Lovallo/Sibony, 2010; Schoemaker, 1993).

"Overconfidence bias" leads decision makers to overestimate their skill and ability to influence future outcomes (Lovallo/Sibony, 2010). As a result, they fail to collect important information or they estimate the time needed for projects incorrectly (Russo/Schoemaker, 1989). Such mistakes can lead to substantial additional costs, especially when they occur in strategic decisions. Overconfidence bias probably played a role in Porsche's 2005 attempt to acquire Volkswagen, a company 15 times its size. The management clearly overestimated its own abilities as well as the financial capacity of Porsche. Ultimately the takeover bid was unsuccessful; instead, Volkswagen acquired Porsche.

"Framing bias" – the second important bias – leads decision makers to change their preferences depending on the way in which a problem is presented (Hodgkinson et al., 1999). Thus, their decision depends on whether gains or losses are highlighted (Kahneman/Tversky, 1984). Framing bias has a negative effect on the quality of decisions (Camerer, 2000) as it changes decision makers' attitude to risk, resulting in irrational decision making. In practice, this means that managers take bigger risks. It likewise has an effect on strategic decisions by managers, as facts are not evaluated rationally. Framing bias is also found for customers: Levin (1987) shows that shoppers evaluate meat products significantly better with regard to quality and taste when the same content is labeled "75% lean" as opposed to "25% fat" (Levin, 1987).

Interest in methods for reducing bias or "debiasing" the decision-making process is growing (Larrick, 2004). However, only a limited amount of research has been produced to date on tools for reducing bias and hence directly improving the quality of decisions. Few of these debiasing methods have been tested empirically (Milkman et al., 2009). The methods in question are largely based on psychological research, and include cognitive mapping (Hodgkinson et al., 1999), "considering the opposite" (Mussweiler et al., 2000), group decision making (Lerner/Tetlock, 1999) and integrating feedback (Fischhoff, 1982).

Research in the area of behavioral strategy has adapted these debiasing methods to meet the requirements of strategic management. This has made them easier to apply in decision-making processes in corporate practice. The methods contain four key elements:
1. Examine decisions through multiple frames, i.e. frame decisions in a number of different ways when considering them (Wright/Goodwin, 2002)
2. Formulate alternatives and contradictory viewpoints (Lovallo/Sibony, 2010)
3. Consider assumptions previously disregarded or ignored (Larrick, 2004)
4. Discuss major uncertainties (Lovallo/Sibony, 2010)

To summarize, integrating debiasing methods into the strategic decision process is critical for increasing the quality of decisions and the performance of companies. By applying the methods outlined above, managers can achieve more rational and less biased decisions.

6.4
AN INTEGRATIVE MODEL OF DECISION QUALITY

We saw above that the three key drivers of decision quality are that decisions must be fast, comprehensive and unbiased. In this section, we combine these drivers and propose an integrative model of decision quality. This model shows us what is important for organizations when designing their decision-making processes.

The design of the decision-making process is a core factor in increasing decision quality and hence the performance of organizations (Lovallo/Sibony, 2010). In addition, comprehensive, quick and unbiased decision making has been shown to increase decision quality and performance (Fredrickson, 1984; Eisenhardt, 1989; Milkman et al., 2009). An optimal decision process should thus combine all three qualities: it should be comprehensive, quick and unbiased.

Previous research has shown that in order to be comprehensive, the decision-making process should include a wide variety of alternatives (Fredrickson, 1984) and involve a high level of investigatory activity (Miller, 2008). Moreover, decision makers should create these multiple alternatives simultaneously (Eisenhardt, 1989) and with a low degree of formalization (Wally/Baum, 1994). Bias can be removed by ensuring that decisions are examined through multiple frames (Wright/Goodwin, 2002) and by formulating alternatives and contradictory viewpoints (Lovallo/Sibony, 2010). In addition, assumptions previously disregarded or ignored should be considered (Larrick, 2004) and major uncertainties in the industry discussed (Lovallo/Sibony, 2010) during the course of the decision-making process. A decision-making process that follows these guidelines should result in better decisions (see Figure 6.1).

6.5 SCENARIO-BASED STRATEGIC PLANNING

Scenario-based strategic planning appears to provide a sound methodological foundation for implementing the process outlined above in corporate practice. Using this approach, organizations can develop scenarios and derive strategies in a period of four to six weeks. The approach is currently used in various industries and is easy to apply thanks to its tool-based design.

One company that has used scenario-based planning to great effect is British Airways (Moyer, 1996). After numerous workshops and a comprehensive planning process, the company gained better insights into changes in its external

FIGURE 6.1: INTEGRATIVE MODEL OF DECISION QUALITY

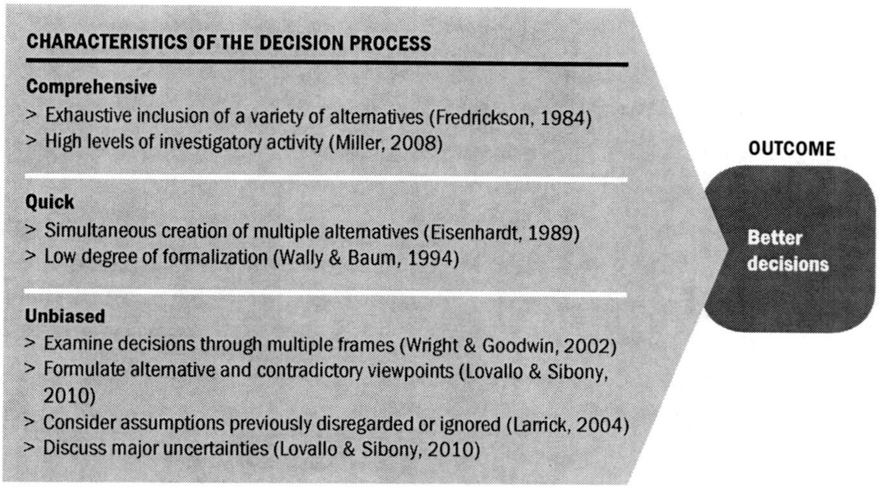

CHARACTERISTICS OF THE DECISION PROCESS

Comprehensive
> Exhaustive inclusion of a variety of alternatives (Fredrickson, 1984)
> High levels of investigatory activity (Miller, 2008)

Quick
> Simultaneous creation of multiple alternatives (Eisenhardt, 1989)
> Low degree of formalization (Wally & Baum, 1994)

Unbiased
> Examine decisions through multiple frames (Wright & Goodwin, 2002)
> Formulate alternative and contradictory viewpoints (Lovallo & Sibony, 2010)
> Consider assumptions previously disregarded or ignored (Larrick, 2004)
> Discuss major uncertainties (Lovallo & Sibony, 2010)

OUTCOME

Better decisions

environment. It was then able to communicate and use the results across all organizational levels of the company (Ringland, 2006).

Scenario-based strategic planning has four main characteristics enabling managers to increase comprehensiveness and speed in the decision-making process and at the same time reducing the negative impact of cognitive biases. These four characteristics combine the qualities of the decision-making process identified by previous researchers as a way of achieving comprehensive, quick and unbiased decisions (Fredrickson, 1984; Miller, 2008; Eisenhardt, 1989; Wally/Baum, 1994; Wright/Goodwin, 2002; Larrick, 2004; Lovallo/Sibony, 2010).

First, in the perception analysis process step, scenario-based planning combines the internal perspective of management with the external perspective of various stakeholder groups. The viewpoints of top management are challenged and confronted with new ideas that had been previously disregarded or perceived incorrectly. This opens up management's thinking and forces them to confront potential blind spots and weak signals. The process step builds on a holistic approach that brings together the perceptions of multiple internal and external stakeholders, ensuring a sufficient level of investigatory activity (Miller, 2008).

Second, scenario-based strategic planning involves developing multiple scenarios (Schoemaker, 1993). By identifying and discussing key areas of uncertainty (Lovallo/Sibony, 2010), decision makers draw up four distinct scenarios. These scenarios allow them to consider a broader range of possible future developments and hence examine the strategic decision through multiple frames.

Third, various different strategic options are developed on the basis of the proposed scenarios during the strategy development phase. These options include strategic plans for specific scenarios as well as a core strategy that is applicable in all scenarios and can be implemented instantly. The different options are derived simultaneously, so speed is not sacrificed to comprehensiveness (Eisenhardt, 1989).

Fourth, scenario-based strategic planning is not based on a single process step but on a series of steps. Its clear structure and tool-based design make it quick and easy for companies to apply. Despite being formalized in the sense of providing tools and frameworks for the different process steps, the workshops and discussions between project team and top management are a crucial ingredient in ensuring that the right level of reflection and strategic thinking takes place to break through fixed mindsets (Hodgkinson et al., 1999). The approach thus combines the methodological rigor needed to effectively gather and manage information with the freedom and low level of formalization involved in discussing and evaluating the results in workshops. The different characteristics of the approach work in combination rather than singly to increase comprehensiveness and speed while combating bias (see Figure 6.2).

Scenario-based strategic planning thus appears to bridge the gap between comprehensive planning for changes in the organization's environment and the ability to adapt to these changes quickly (Schoemaker, 2002; Wiltbank et al., 2006). At the same time, it appears to overcome the cognitive barriers that can reduce

FIGURE 6.2: BENEFITS OF SCENARIO-BASED PLANNING

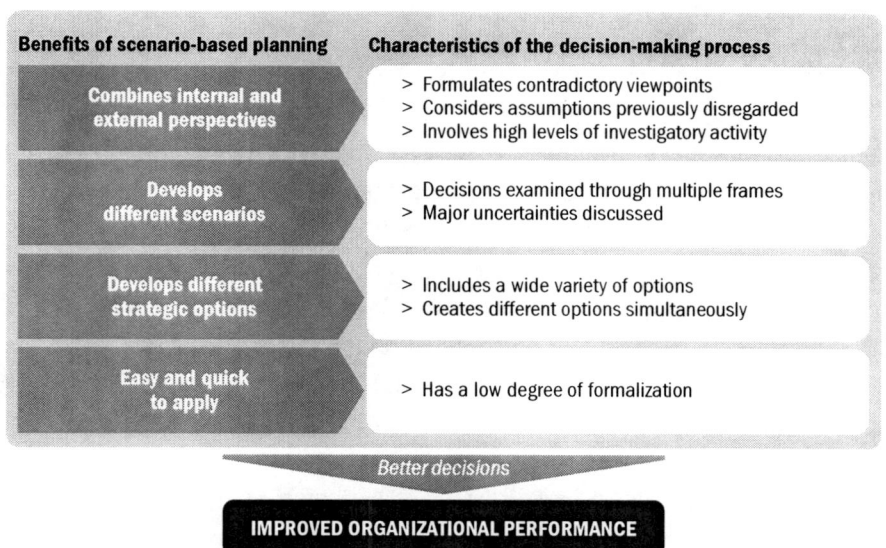

decision quality. Initial empirical findings support this assumption. Schoemaker (1993) and Bradfield (2008) show that scenario planning has the potential to reduce overconfidence bias: decision makers showed significantly lower levels of overconfidence bias after conducting a scenario exercise (Schoemaker, 1993). The same is found for "confirmation bias", or the tendency to look at and evaluate new information in such a way that existing assumptions and beliefs are confirmed and potential counterarguments disproved (Bazerman/Moore, 2009). Bradfield (2008) demonstrates in a case study that applying scenario planning overcomes this bias also.

From our conceptual analysis and review of initial empirical findings, it thus appears that scenario-based strategic planning is a useful method of improving the quality of decisions in corporate practice. It provides an open and multi-dimensional approach to strategic planning and decision making that fosters strategic thinking (van der Heijden, 2005), reduces biased judgments (Schoemaker, 1993) and combines rational decision-making comprehensiveness with increased adaptability (Schoemaker, 2002). These factors both increase the speed of the decision-making process itself and the time taken to react to changes in an organization's environment.

6.6 CONCLUSION

Scenario-based strategic planning has great potential to increase the quality of decisions and companies' performance, especially in today's turbulent and uncertain business conditions (Chermack, 2011). Above, we propose an integrated model that analyzes the process characteristics based on which high-quality decisions can be achieved in corporate practice. We have also seen how scenario-based strategic planning provides a methodological foundation for implementing such a decision-making process, increasing comprehensiveness and speed at the same time as reducing the negative effects of cognitive biases.

Our findings have important implications for future research, as well as for corporate practice. Initial empirical research has taken place into debiasing (Schoemaker, 1993; Bradfield, 2008) but the influence of scenario planning on comprehensiveness and speed has yet to be analyzed empirically. Nor have researchers carried out empirical studies on the impact of scenario planning on the quality of decisions. This opens up some promising avenues for future research.

With respect to corporate practice, our findings have implications for the effective design of decision-making processes in companies. Using scenario-based strategic planning as a standard strategic planning tool may also enhance the quality of decisions by improving the overall strategy process.

Scenario-based planning not only potentially changes the behavior and thinking of executives, it can also form the foundation for a more open, flexible and adaptive strategy process that ultimately improves performance. As Blenko et al. (2010) have recently pointed out, effective decision making can increase total shareholder return by six percentage points.

6.7 REFERENCES

Amason AC. 1996. Distinguishing the effects of functional and dysfunctional conflict on strategic decision making: Resolving a paradox for top management teams. *Academy of Management Journal* 39(1): 123-148.

Atuahene-Gima K., Li H. 2004. Strategic decision comprehensiveness and new product development outcomes in new technology ventures. *Academy of Management Journal* 47(4): 583-597.

Bateman TS., Zeithaml CP. 1989a. The psychological context of strategic decisions: A model and convergent experimental findings. *Strategic Management Journal* 10(1): 59-74.

Bateman TS., Zeithaml CP. 1989b. The psychological context of strategic decisions: a test of relevance to practitioners. *Strategic Management Journal* 10(6): 587-592.

Baum JR., Wally S. 2003. Strategic decision speed and firm performance. *Strategic Management Journal* 24(11): 1107-1129.

Bazerman MH., Moore DA. 2009. *Judgment in Managerial Decision Making. Hoboken: John Wiley and Sons.*

Blenko WM., Mankins MC., Rogers P. 2010. The decision-driven organization. *Harvard Business Review* 88(6): 54-62.

Bradfield RM. 2008. Cognitive barriers in the scenario development process. *Advances in Developing Human Resources* 10(2): 198-215.

Bradley SP., Sullivan EE. 2005. AOL Time Warner, Inc. *Harvard Business School Case.*

Braybrooke D., Lindblom CE. 1963. *A Strategy of Decision: Policy Evaluation as a Social Process. New York: Free Press.*

Camerer CF. 2000. *Prospect Theory in the Wild: Evidence from the Field. New York: Russell Sage Foundation.*

Chermack TJ. 2011. *Scenario Planning in Organizations: How to Create, Use, and Assess Scenarios. San Francisco: Berrett-Koehler Publishers.*

Dane E., Pratt MG. 2007. Exploring intuition and its role in managerial decision making. *Academy of Management Review* 32(1): 33-54.

Das TK., Teng BS. 1999. Cognitive biases and strategic decision processes: An integrative perspective. *Journal of Management Studies* 36(6): 757-778.

Dean JW., Sharfman MP. 1996. Does decision process matter? A study of strategic decision-making effectiveness. *Academy of Management Journal* 39(2): 368-396.

Eisenhardt KM. 1989. Making fast strategic decisions in high-velocity environments. *Academy of Management Journal* 32(3): 543-576.

Fischhoff B. 1982. Debiasing. In *Judgment under uncertainty: Heuristics and biases. Kahneman D, Slovic P, Tversky A (eds.). Cambridge: Cambridge University Press: 422-444.*

Forbes DP. 2005. *Managerial determinants of decision speed in new ventures. Strategic Management Journal* 26(4): 355-366.

Forbes DP. 2007. Reconsidering the strategic implications of decision comprehensiveness. *Academy of Management Review* 32(2): 361-376.

Fredrickson JW., Mitchell TR. 1984. Strategic decision processes: Comprehensiveness and Performance in an industry with an unstable environment. *Academy of Management Journal* 27(2): 399-423.

Fredrickson JW. 1984. The comprehensiveness of strategic decision processes: Extension, observations, future directions. *Academy of Management Journal* 27(3): 445-466.

Garvin DA., Levesque LC. 2006. Strategic planning at United Parcel Service. *Harvard Business School Case.*

Glick WH., Miller CC., Huber GP. 1993. *The impact of upper-echelon diversity on organizational performance. In Organizational Change and Redesign: Ideas and Insights for Improving Performance. Huber GP, Glick WH (eds.). New York: Oxford University Press: 178-214.*

Hart S., Banbury C. 1994. *How strategy making processes can make a difference. Strategic Management Journal* 15(4): 251-269.

Healey MP., Hodgkinson GP. 2008. Troubling futures: Scenarios and scenario planning for organizational decision making. In *The Oxford Handbook of Organizational Decision Making, Hodgkinson GP, Starbuck WH (eds.). Oxford: Oxford University Press: 565-585.*

Hodgkinson CD., Bown NJ., Maule AJ., Glaister KW., Pearman AD. 1999. Breaking the frame: An analysis of strategic cognition and decision making under uncertainty. *Strategic Management Journal* 20(10): 977-985.

Hodgkinson GP., Sadler-Smith G., Burke LA., Claxton G., Sparrow PR. 2009. Intuition in organizations: Implications for strategic management. *Long Range Planning* 42(3): 277-297.

Hodgkinson GP., Starbuck WH. 2008. *The Oxford Handbook of Organizational Decision Making.* Oxford: Oxford University Press.

Hough JR., White MA. 2003. Environmental dynamism and strategic decision-making rationality: an examination at the decision level. *Strategic Management Journal* 24(5): 481-489.

Judge WQ., Miller A. 1991. Antecedents and outcomes of decision speed in different environmental contexts. *Academy of Management Journal* 34(2): 449-463.

Kahneman D., Slovic P., Tversky A. 1982. *Judgment Under Uncertainty: Heuristics and Biases.* Cambridge: Cambridge University Press.

Kahneman D., Tversky A. 1984. Choices, values, and frames. *American Psychologist* 39(4): 341-350.

Kahneman D., Tversky A. 2000. *Choices, Values, and Frames.* Cambridge: Cambridge University Press.

Kahneman D., Klein G. 2009. Conditions for intuitive expertise A failure to disagree. *American Psychologist* 64(6): 515-526.

Kahneman D., Klein G. 2010. When can you trust your gut? *McKinsey Quarterly* 10(2): 58-67.

Kahneman D., Lovallo D., Sibony O. 2011. Before you make that big decision. *Harvard Business Review* 89(6): 50-60.

Larrick RP. 2004. Debiasing. In *Blackwell handbook of judgment and decision making.* Koehler DJ, Harvey N (eds.). Oxford: Blackwell: 316-337.

Lerner JS., Tetlock PE. 1999. Accounting for the effects of accountability. *Psychological Bulletin* 125(2): 255-275.

Levin IP. 1987. Associative effects of information framing. *Bulletin of the Psychonomic Society* 25: 85-86.

Lovallo D., Sibony O. 2010. The case for behavioral strategy. *McKinsey Quarterly* 10(2): 30-45.

Milkman KL., Chugh D., Bazerman, MH. 2009. How can decision making be improved? *Perspectives on Psychological Science* 4(4): 378-383.

Miller CC. 2008. Decisional comprehensiveness and firm performance: Towards a more complete understanding. *Journal of Behavioral Decision Making* 21(5): 598-620.

Moyer K. 1996. Scenario planning at British Airways - A case study. *Long Range Planning* 29(2): 172-181.

Mussweiler T., Strack F., Pfeiffer T. 2000. Overcoming the inevitable anchoring effect: Considering the opposite compensate for selective accessibility. *Personality and Social Psychology Bulletin* 26(9): 1142-1150.

Priem RL., Rasheed AMA., Kotulic AG. 1996. Rationality in strategic decision processes, environmental dynamism and firm performance. *Journal of Management* 21(5): 913-929.

Ringland G. 2006. *Scenario Planning: Managing for the Future. Chichester: John Wiley and Sons.*

Schoemaker PJH. 1993. Multiple scenario development: Its conceptual and behavioral foundation. *Strategic Management Journal* 14(3): 193-213.

Schoemaker PJH. 1995. Scenario planning: A tool for strategic thinking. *Sloan Management Review* 37(2): 25-40.

Schoemaker PJH. 2002. *Profiting from Uncertainty: Strategies for Succeeding No Matter What the Future Brings. New York: The Free Press.*

Stevenson H., Gumpert D. 1985. The heart of entrepreneurship. *Harvard Business Review* 63(2): 85-94.

Tversky A., Kahneman D. 1974. Judgment under uncertainty: Heuristics and biases. *Science* 185(4157): 1124-1131.

Tversky A., Kahneman D. 1981. The framing of decisions and the psychology of choice. *Science* 211(4481): 453-458.

van der Heijden K. 2005. *Scenarios: The Art of Strategic Conversation. Chichester: John Wiley and Sons.*

Wack P. 1985a. Scenarios: Uncharted waters ahead. *Harvard Business Review* 63(5): 73-89.

Wack P. 1985b. Scenarios: Shooting the Rapids. *Harvard Business Review* 63(6): 139-150.

Wally S., Baum JR. 1994. Personal and structural determinants of the pace of strategic decision making. *Academy of Management Journal* 37(4): 932-956.

Walters BA., Bhuian SN. 2004. Complexity absorption and performance: A structural analysis of acute-care hospitals. *Journal of Management* 30(1): 97-121.

Wiltbank R., Dew N., Read S., Sarasvathy SD. 2006. What to do next? The case for non-predictive strategy. *Strategic Management Journal* 27(10): 981-998.

Wright G., Goodwin P. 2002. Eliminating a framing bias by using simple instructions to 'think harder' and respondents with managerial experience: comment on 'breaking the frame'. *Strategic Management Journal* 23(11): 1059-1067.

7. The benefits of scenario-based planning

How scenario-based planning fosters flexible strategies

CORNELIA GEISSLER, CHRISTIAN KRYS

SCENARIO-BASED STRATEGIC PLANNING

In the last chapter we saw how scenario-based planning can improve decision processes. We will now turn our attention to decisions at an aggregated or corporate level. We will examine how entire strategies can change and – ideally – be optimized. The key question is how scenario-based planning can help make strategies more flexible. This chapter therefore begins by explaining what exactly is meant by "flexible strategies" and where they belong in the conceptual scheme of things. We will look at factors that impair the flexibility of a company's strategies and suggest ways to overcome these hindrances. Examples drawn from various industries illustrate why and in what areas today's businesses depend more heavily than ever on flexible strategies.

7.1 INTRODUCTION

Realigning a global organization is a major undertaking. Again and again, though, companies find that timely self-reinvention puts fresh wind in their sails. To put that another way: If you can't change, you can't seize opportunities. Why? Because precisely this inability, this *immobility*, incurs opportunity costs and blunts a firm's competitive edge. Flexibility, on the other hand, can increase the value of the company, create competitive advantages and thus contribute to both growth and successful performance.

Take the example of Korea's Samsung Group. Long looked down on as a cheap-and-cheerful electronics producer, it has now evolved into a leading high-tech provider known for its outstanding research and development work (Khanna et al., 2011). Finnish mobile phone vendor Nokia has likewise reinvented its portfolio several times over – moving from rubber products to televisions to mobile handsets – and has successfully established a new market positioning every time. Failure to factor the trend toward smartphones into its strategy quickly enough has now once again brought the company to a turning point in its development. US technology group IBM is another major player that is known for its self-transformation capabilities, having morphed from a maker of mainframe hardware to an integrated provider of software, service and consulting. These examples show that flexibility and long-term strategies go hand in hand. It is no longer enough just to tweak individual functions if you want to respond to profound changes in the marketplace – you need to see the bigger picture. Flexibility is not a strategy in itself. Regardless, companies do well to strive toward the integrated, strategic planning of enterprise flexibility (Meffert, 1999).

7.2
STRATEGIC FLEXIBILITY – OPENING THE DOOR TO A CHANGE OF STRATEGY

Strategic flexibility addresses the issue of what conditions must be put in place and what must be done to enable a company to apply a change of strategy. The changeover happens when a company formulates and implements a new strategy (in the context of business process reengineering, restructuring, realignment or a turnaround, for example). The process is accompanied by the adaptation of organizational structures, information systems, the corporate culture and staff incentives (Burmann, 2004a). It follows that strategic flexibility is not limited to certain periods or phases of corporate development.

There is no shortage of related concepts. Agility, resilience, transformative and adaptive capacity, dynamic capabilities, flexibility: Literature on the subject uses all these terms to describe the attributes a company must possess if it is to survive in a volatile competitive environment. The definitions, however, are not exactly clear-cut. Some concepts place greater emphasis on resources or processes. Others focus on the cognitive aspect: those factors that concern the behavior of managers and employees. Some of the most important concepts are described in this section.

The extent of a company's "strategic agility" shows how flexible its strategy process is (Doz/Kosonen, 2008). Agility can be seen as a combination of three capabilities:
- Strategic sensitivity: The ability to open up the strategy process and create a multidimensional organization by involving key internal and external stakeholders
- Leadership unity: Top management's ability to act as a team. Its job is not to dictate the answers, but to create a context that is conducive to collaborative work

- Resource fluidity: The ability to quickly make financial and human resources available where they are needed most. This means dismantling bureaucracy, overcoming silo mentalities and introducing modular process structures

"Strategic resilience" is the term used to describe the ability to reinvent business models and strategies when conditions and circumstances change. Companies should be put in a position where they can anticipate any form of change that poses a threat to their most important sources of profitability – and to respond before problems materialize (Hamel/Välikangas, 2003). In other words, strategic resilience enables a company to launch robust change initiatives in response to specific situations in order to safeguard its long-term survival in the marketplace (Lengnick-Hall/Beck, 2009).

The terms "transformative" and "adaptive capacity" focus on the technology side. They refer to a company's ability to constantly redefine its product portfolio by drawing on technological opportunities both outside (adaptive capacity) and inside the firm (transformative capacity), thereby giving itself a competitive advantage (Garud/Nayyar, 1994).

Most of these approaches share the same conceptual roots: They all highlight a company's strategic agility from the resource and competence angle. From the perspective of the resource based view, strategic agility – and hence a company's lasting success – is linked to the appropriate redistribution of existing resources and the addition of new ones. As far back as the 1950s, resource theorists sought to use the interplay of resource accumulation and reorganization to explain the phenomenon of long-term growth (Penrose, 1959). At the end of the 1990s, the dynamic capabilities theory took over where this idea left off. Scholars no longer looked to growth as the measure of success, but to a firm's ability to carve out different competitive advantages. Teece, Pisano and Shuen defined the term "dynamic capabilities": "... dynamic capabilities [are] ... the firm's ability to integrate, build, and reconfigure internal and external competences to address rapidly changing environments. Dynamic capabilities thus reflect an organization's ability to achieve new and innovative forms of competitive advantage given path dependencies and market positions" (Teece et al., 1997, p. 516).

FIGURE 7.1: STRATEGIC FLEXIBILITY AS A META-CAPABILITY

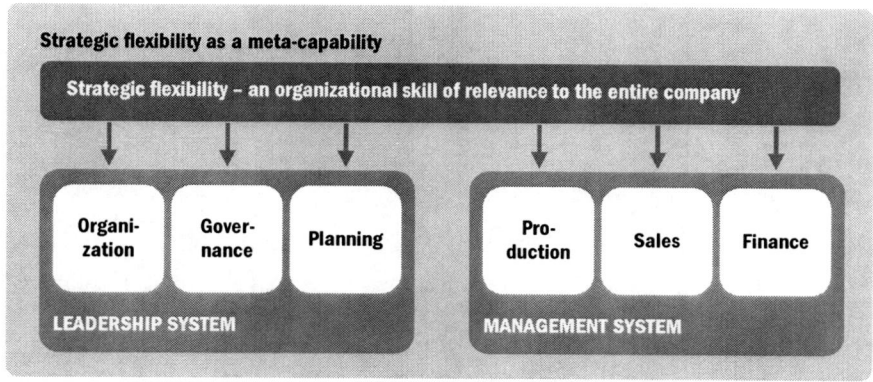

Source: Burmann, 2004a

Dynamic capabilities, then, are enterprise-wide competences that link ongoing processes to an organization's historic development and its endowment with resources (Burmann, 2004b). These are the capabilities that keep a company and its strategy flexible. But what exactly does that mean? Let us take a closer look at the term "strategic flexibility".

According to the Latin root, a thing is flexible if it is pliable, supple and adaptable. If they are bent in a given direction, flexible physical objects can often be returned to their original form. Not so the change in an organization, which is permanent. So if strategic flexibility is to be based on dynamic capabilities, it must be seen as a meta-capability that embraces the entire enterprise and all its functional units.

Flexibility depends on the extent to which and the way in which an organization can be guided at all or, conversely, what self-guiding dynamics it develops as a system. It also depends on how agile an organization is. In this context, it is important to clarify what conditions are in place to enable the company to maintain strategic flexibility, what obstacles might still be in place and how they can be eliminated (Volberda, 1999). Such conditions can include incentive structures for the relevant parties, organizational structures and processes, financial and cost elasticity and criteria relating to the target market.

Strategic options can be exploited to the full only if these factors of influence are fully visible and optimized.

7.3
OBSTACLES TO STRATEGIC FLEXIBILITY

There is always an inherent tension whenever strategic change takes place. The need for order, organization and control on the one hand pulls against the need for rapid response, dynamic learning processes and change on the other. As we saw in chapter 2, forecasting the outcome of profound and ongoing change is not easy to do, which makes it hard to get the strategy process moving in the right direction. The challenge is therefore to design strategic processes that have sufficient built-in flexibility. So what obstacles to strategic flexibility might one encounter?

Let us briefly examine the forces of inertia that prevail in many organizations. The following mechanisms can render strategies inflexible:

Inertia is the inability to set new internal processes in motion in response to changes in external conditions (Miller/Friesen, 1980; Tushman/Romanelli, 1985). The causes of inertia tend to be inflexible social structures, cognitive styles that have become encrusted, rigid behavioral patterns and proven decision heuristics (Volberda/Baden-Fuller, 1998). A company can, for example, become inert if its resources are closely tied to defined strategic initiatives. If the prevailing conditions change, such resources cannot readily be reallocated from one strategic initiative to another. The reasons for the inflexibility of resources may be endogenous (where an extensive resource pool or a large number of direct reports gives rise to power struggles, for example). But they might equally be exogenous and driven, say, by resource markets.

The classic example is capital: It will always be easier to raise capital for a business model that manifestly already works than for risky new ventures.

A company's strong market position can also hinder the reallocation of resources to new business lines. In many cases, there is simply no incentive for management to forfeit a powerful market position in established lines in favor of an alternative that is fraught with uncertainty.

CASE STUDY: EASTMAN KODAK

In retrospect, Eastman Kodak is regarded as the Google of its day (The Economist, 2012). Kodak pioneered both ground-breaking technologies and marketing innovations. In 1976, the company accounted for an astonishing 90% of the US market for film materials and 85% of the US market for cameras. Even in the 1990s, the company was still singled out as one of the five most valuable brands in the world for several years running (The Economist, 2012). Its rival Fuji enjoyed a similar position on the Japanese market.

When the market moved on from analog to digital photography, however, margins slumped, threatening the business models of both Kodak and Fuji.

As early as 1981, when rival Sony launched "Mavica", the first ever digital camera, an internal analysis at Kodak rated the potential of digital photography as very high. The market transition was accelerated by the fact that China's fast-growing middle class quite simply leapfrogged analog photography altogether. However, Kodak's margins on films, chemicals and development were still so fat that it refused to alter its course. The company's lack of adaptability had fatal consequences for its stock price and its ongoing development (Caroll/Mui, 2008). Eventually, in January 2012 Kodak filed for chapter 11 business reorganization.

Rigid routines within the organization also contribute to inertia in decision processes. Routines are reactions that occur automatically or rules that govern decision outcomes, linking different activities to each other. While some are institutionalized, others go largely unnoticed by the members of an organization. Working through defined project phases in a straight line is just one example. Once established, however, such routine organizational processes are very difficult to change (Gilbert, 2005).

Different types of internal reactionary force can keep a company on a strategic development trajectory for a long time. That is not necessarily a bad thing, because the benefits of experience and organizational learning can improve efficiency and strengthen the firm's competitive position. At the same time, however, what are known as path dependencies can prevent strategic realignment by creating lock-in effects, and it is not unusual for these effects to impair flexibility in the long run. A company that seems to be running on rails can quickly find itself shunted into the sidings. Unquestioning adherence to strategies and processes that have served the company well in the past can be difficult to uproot if and when a change of strategy becomes necessary.

Path dependencies usually begin with a critical incident followed by a series of decisions that are reinforced by positive feedback. This process is often illustrated using the QWERTY keyboard on modern PCs. This keyboard layout was originally selected by the inventor of the typewriter to compensate for mechanical deficiencies. When the computer age dawned, however, it was retained without question. Proposals for a more ergonomic layout made eminent sense, but failed to become established.

7.4
PRACTICAL APPLICATION

This section looks at case studies from a number of industries. Their purpose is to show the points at which various companies needed, adopted or missed out on strategic flexibility. What becomes clear is that flexibility can play a number of widely differing roles in corporate strategy processes.

◆ **Power generation**: In Germany, the government's unexpectedly abrupt withdrawal from nuclear energy is forcing energy producers to alter their strategies. Accelerated in the wake of the Fukushima nuclear disaster, this shift in energy policy drove many utilities into the red. The new situation therefore demands a strategic realignment, as old business models will become non-viable in the medium term. Existing resources cannot be reallocated at the drop of a hat, however: Power companies have already invested in plants and processes to generate nuclear energy, tying up their capital for decades to come. To make matters worse, there are still no reliable guidelines on which realignment might be based. Decisions have still not been made on political conditions surrounding the promotion of energy from renewable sources, the permanent disposal of radioactive material and the time frame for further expansion of the power grid. New strategies are therefore needed that will work irrespective of these uncertainties.

Storage technologies for alternative forms of energy could be one possibility. Hybrid power plants, for example, use electrolysis to generate hydrogen and oxygen from excess electricity from wind turbines. The hydrogen is then separated from the oxygen and stored, transforming volatile electricity into an energy-rich gas that can readily be stored. New cooperative ventures are needed for the project. In one such venture, wind power company Enertrag has teamed up with petroleum company Total, power utility Vattenfall and German rail carrier Deutsche Bahn. The total cost is EUR 21 million (Dambeck, 2011).

- **Automotive engineering**: While the political arena is called on to respond at short notice to unforeseen events, megatrends are the driving force behind changes in the strategic environment in the corporate sector. When several such megatrends converge, the resultant transition can be profound indeed. The auto industry is a fine example: The closer attention commanded by sustainability, technological advances (in e-mobility, telematic systems and networking, for example) and scarce resources will radically alter OEMs' business models in the years ahead (Wendt, 2011).

For decades, the automotive industry focused its attention on pumping money into production facilities, dimensioning production to maximize capacity utilization and flooding the market with more and more new variants of cost-optimized standard models, many of them at knock-down prices. This practice still works in the fast-growing Chinese and Indian markets. In the industrialized world, however, auto makers have to morph into mobility service providers. In these traditional markets, the automobile's sheen as a status symbol has become noticeably tarnished.

New mobility models, the integration of IT service providers and energy suppliers, in-car apps and new customer demands in terms of mobility and networking are necessitating huge investments in IT, infrastructure and the development of new, efficient solutions. This kind of model links a new form of automobility (based on

FIGURE 7.2: IMPACT OF FIVE MEGA-TRENDS ON THE AUTOMOTIVE INDUSTRY

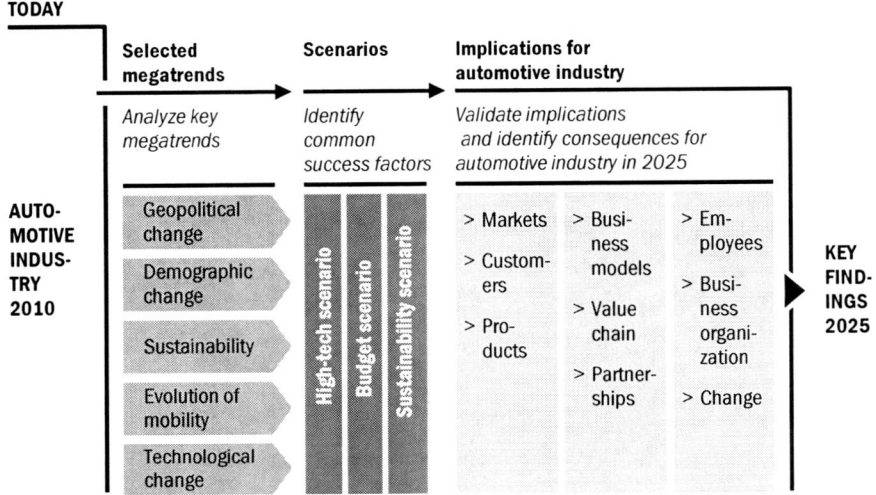

Source: Wendt, 2011

use instead of ownership) to seamless, barrier-free transitions between private vehicular traffic, public transportation and non-motorized forms of transportation. The key issue is to organize three scarce resources – energy, space and time – in such a way that urban development can be made livable, functional and sustainable at the same time (Schmidt, 2011a).

◆ **Media**: The media sector has been in structural transition for years. The advance of digital technology, accompanied by new user habits and convergence of the telecommunications, IT and media markets, is having a disruptive effect on the business models of traditional providers. Many traditional media companies have yet to find suitable responses. The US newspaper market, for example, has been languishing in crisis for years. The New York Times – the publication of choice for the global intelligentsia – saw its annual sales slump by 27% from USD 3.3 billion to USD 2.4 billion from 2006 to 2011 (Schmidt, 2011b). Nor is there any sign that the transition is slowing down. The number of Internet users worldwide has now exceeded two billion, whereas only 250 million people around the globe enjoyed Internet connectivity as recently as the year 2000.

The initial strategy adopted by many media companies – offering free content on digital platform – has failed. On the American dailies market, free and unlimited use of websites and mobile offerings has mostly been abandoned. Access to the third-biggest newspaper in the US (again the New York Times) costs at least USD 15 for four weeks or USD 195 a year (Schmidt, 2011b).

Media companies need ways to diversify if they are to soften their dependency on content business that is funded by advertising as quickly as possible. The Axel Springer media group, for example, generated more than one third of its revenues online in 2011. And most of that was not made with journalistic content, but with the Stepstone online job exchange and the Immonet and Seloger real estate marketplaces, for example. The company is thus evolving from a traditional publisher to an Internet service provider (Bernau, 2012).

7.5
SCENARIO-BASED PLANNING AS A TOOL TO CRAFT STRATEGIC FLEXIBILITY

Strategy research assumes that some aspects of strategy processes evolve without any conscious planning. That, however, can be no excuse for tolerating suboptimal processes. Scenario-based planning can help a company overcome the inertia and lock-in effects that arise from path dependencies. In this context, strategic flexibility is a concept that helps to visualize **potential** courses of action (Burmann, 2004b) and thereby enables managers to make the most of the strategic options at their disposal.

The scenario method is a perfect complement to the strategy process, opening it up both within the company and toward the outside world. First and foremost, this method ensures that representatives of all a company's functional units are involved in the strategy process. It also gives the organization a keener perception of the relevant exogenous influences, by also calling in external stakeholders to identify relevant factors of influence. Asking open questions at the start of the 360° stakeholder feedback stage makes sure that strategic planning does not become too

FIGURE 7.3: DIMENSIONS OF STRATEGIC FLEXIBILITY

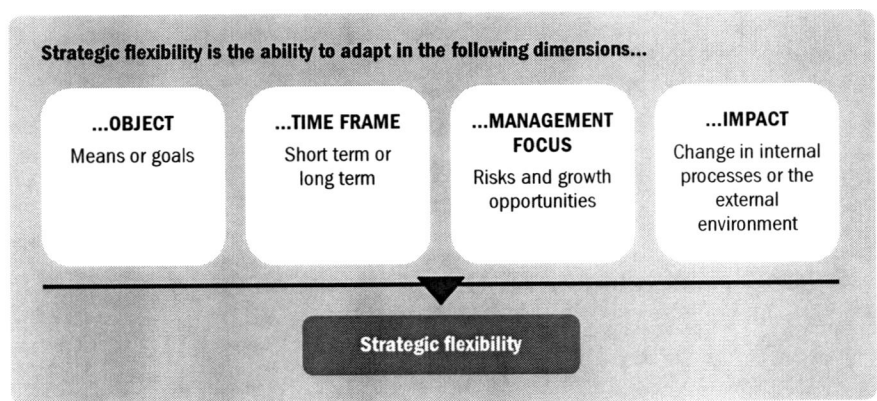

Source: Burmann, 2004b

heavily focused on specific dimensions (such as the object, time frame or impact) at too early a stage. Instead, it allows influences to be explored initially with no consideration for any cause-and-effect relationships. Four dimensions outline the potential for action:

The first dimension examines flexibility with regard to the goals the company wants to achieve and the means it intends to employ to do so. The following permutations are possible:
- A new weighting is given to existing goals
- New goals (such as sustainability and diversity) are added
- The deployment of factors of production such as capital and human resources changes (in both qualitative and quantitative terms)

The second dimension describes the time frame that an organization can consider when changing its strategic alignment. The spectrum ranges from
- The short-term reshuffle of existing resources to

- The long-term reallocation of the resource portfolio in light of anticipated future demand based on a new delivery program

The third dimension measures how flexible the management is in terms of the options available to it. Management can
- operate a defensive/passive risk strategy to guard against risks (by monitoring KPIs and comparing to past values, for example)
- actively and aggressively seek new growth opportunities and be prepared to quickly modify its structures and processes
- be flexible with regard to speed and readiness to act

The fourth dimension looks at the impact environmental factors have on the flexibility of organizations. In particular:
- The specific influence on market conditions (by launching innovations, for example)
- The change in internal process variables, optimization and streamlining

Each of these four dimensions can be supported by our method of scenario-based strategic planning. For example, 360° stakeholder feedback contributes to finding new goals and adjusting the weight of existing goals. The impact/uncertainty grid can help assess the influence of market conditions or changes in process variables.

Scenario-based planning can overcome forces of inertia within the organization and break up (or help redirect) well-worn development paths. Via positive feedback loops, the range of strategic actions is narrowed over time. As long as the overall environment is stable, there is no difficulty reducing the options to a single path. But if the environment changes, lock-in effects can occur, placing strategic flexibility and competitiveness at risk. The scenario method can then re-open the strategic planning process and break up existing paths.

These insights can also be mapped onto higher levels of strategic planning, as behavioral patterns take shape on the basis of such decisions. Lock-in effects narrow the frame of reference within which strategic options are analyzed. They also limit the scope of management initiatives and ultimately lead to strategically inefficient outcomes (Schreyögg et al., 2003).

FIGURE 7.4: IMPACT OF THE SCENARIO METHOD ON LOCK-INS IN STRATEGIC PLANNING

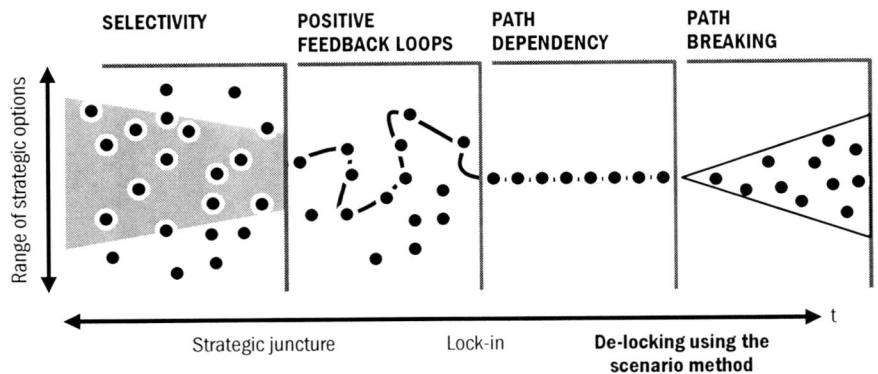

Source: Schreyögg et al., 2003

The method can be used to generate momentum that helps alternative courses of action make the breakthrough. Applied consistently, the scenario method will ideally prevent strategic options from ever becoming excessively restricted. It can do this because, irrespective of existing strategic priorities, it explicitly seeks out weak signals and blind spots.

7.6 REFERENCES

Bernau V. 2012. Dienstleister statt Verleger. Springer macht sein Geld im Netz. *Süddeutsche Zeitung* 08.03.2012, 21.

Burmann C. 2004a. *Strategische Flexibilität und Strategiewechsel als Determinanten des Unternehmenswertes.* Wiesbaden: Gabler.

Burmann C. 2004b. Strategische Flexibilität und der Marktwert von Unternehmen. In *Erfolgsfaktor Flexibilität.* Kaluza B., Becker T. (eds.). Berlin: Erich Schmidt Verlag: 29-53.

Collins DJ., Montgomery CA. 1994. Competing on Resources. *Harvard Business Review* 73(7/8): 118-128.

Dambeck H. 2011. Wind im Tank. *Spiegel Online*. http://www.spiegel.de/wissenschaft/technik/0,1518,793840,00.html. Accessed 13 March 2012.

Doz Y., Kosonen M. 2008. Fast Strategy– How strategic agility will help you to stay ahead of the game. *Strategy Magazine* 15(3), 6-10.

Garud R., Nayyar PR. 1994. Transformative capacity: Continual structuring by intertemporal technology transfer. *Strategic Management Journal* 15(5): 365-385.

Gilbert CG. 2005. Unbundling the structure of inertia. Resource versus routine rigidity. *Academy of Management Journal* 48(5): 741–763.

Hamel G., Välikangas L. 2003. The quest for resilience. *Harvard Business Review* 81(9): 52-65.

Hannan MT., Freeman J. 1984: Structural inertia and organizational change. *American Sociological Review* 49(2): 149-164.

Jacob H. 1989. Flexibilität und ihre Bedeutung für die Betriebspolitik. In *Integration und Flexibilität*. Adam D., Backhaus K., Meffert H., Wagner H. (eds.). Wiesbaden: Gabler: 15-60.

Katsuhiko S., Hitt MA. 2004. Strategic flexibility: Organizational preparedness to reverse ineffective strategic decisions. *Academy of Management Executive* 18(4): 44-59.

Khanna T., Song J., Kyungmook L. 2011: The paradox of Samsung's rise. *Harvard Business Review* 89(7): 142–147.

Kaluza B. 1993. Flexibilität, betriebliche. In *Handwörterbuch der Betriebswirtschaft*. Wittmann W. et al. (eds.). Stuttgart: Schaeffer-Poeschel: 1174-1183.

Lengnick-Hall CA., Beck TE. 2009. Resilience Capacity and Strategic Agility: Prerequisites for Thriving in a Dynamic Environment. The University of Texas at San Antonio, *College of Business Working Paper Series*. http://business.utsa.edu/wps/mgt/0059MGT-199-2009.pdf. Accessed 13 March 2012.

Meffert H. 1985. Größere Flexibilität als Unternehmenskonzept. *Zeitschrift für betriebswirtschaftliche Forschung*. 37(2): 121-137.

Miller D., Friesen PH. 1980. Momentum and revolution in organizational adaptation. *Academy of Management Journal* 23(4), 591-614.

Penrose E. 1959. *The theory of the growth of the firm.* New York and Oxford: Oxford University Press.

Schmidt, A. (Ed.). 2011b. Intelligence on wheels. *think:act Business COO Insights.* Roland Berger Strategy Consultants. 2/2011: 21-23.

Schmidt, A. (Ed.). 2011b. Can print survive the Internet? *think:act Business COO Insights.* Roland Berger Strategy Consultants. 2/2011: 24-27.

Schreyögg G., Sydow J., Koch J. 2003: Organisatorische Pfade – Von der Pfadabhängigkeit zur Pfadkreation. In *Strategische Prozesse und Pfade.* Schreyögg J., Sydow J. (eds.). Wiesbaden: Gabler: 258-294.

Sydow J., Schreyögg G., Koch J. 2009. Organizational path dependence: Opening the black box. *Academy of Management Review* 34(4): 689–709.

The Economist. 2012. Technological change: The last Kodak moment? *The Economist* 402(8767): 63-64.

Teece DJ., Pisano G., Shuen, A. 1997. Dynamic capabilities and strategic Management. *Strategic Management Journal* 18(7): 509-533.

Tushman ML., Romanelli E. 1985. Organizational evolution: A metamorphosis model of convergence and reorientation. In *Research in organizational behavior* (Vol. 7). Cummings, LL, Staw BM (eds.). Greenwich: JAI Press: 171–122.

Volberda HW. 1997. Building flexible organizations for fast-moving markets. *Long Range Planning* 30(2): 169-183.

Volberda HW., Baden-Fuller C. 1998. Strategic Renewal and competence building. Four dynamic mechanisms. In *Strategic Flexibility: Managing in a Turbulent Economy.* Hamel G., Prahalad CK, Thomas H., O'Neal V. (eds.) Chichester: Wiley: 371-389.

Wendt T. 2011. *Automotive landscape 2025.* Roland Berger Strategy Consultants study. http://www.rolandberger.com/media/press/releases/511-press_archive2011_sc_content/Automotive-landscape-2025.html. Accessed 13 March 2012.

8. Conclusion – Good management and scenario planning

BURKHARD SCHWENKER, TORSTEN WULF

SCENARIO-BASED STRATEGIC PLANNING

This book introduces the HHL-Roland Berger approach to scenario-based strategic planning – an approach that helps planners manage complexity, volatility and uncertainty in the strategy process. This final chapter summarizes the challenges to good management and shows how scenario planning can help managers overcome them.

8.1
THE CHALLENGES OF GOOD MANAGEMENT TODAY

When we started developing the HHL-Roland Berger approach to scenario-based strategic planning back in 2009, the financial crisis was just reaching its peak and there was no indication of how long the crisis would last. In the event, Germany recovered quickly – although how long the recovery will last is equally unclear. What *is* clear is that we will not return to a long period of sustained economic certainty and stable growth. The uncertainty ushered in by the crisis is here to stay.

In the second chapter of this book we looked at the reasons behind this prolonged uncertainty. In particular, we saw that:
1. Volatility will continue to be high, both within companies and in the environment at large
2. The complexity stemming from the need to consider multiple dimensions in the strategic planning process will grow
3. Ambiguity will remain, as the variables involved in strategic decisions and their exact role remain unclear

These phenomena give rise to certain contradictions that all good managers these days must face. (For a detailed discussion, refer to the book "On Good Management" by Schwenker and Müller-Dofel, 2013):
- The future is complex and unpredictable. Even so – or perhaps precisely because this is so – employees feel a need for security.
- Experience shows that trends shift into reverse and forecasts often miss the mark. Yet companies still have to plan, do their sums and decide about investments.
- An interdisciplinary mindset – the ability to combine economic and business management concepts, social and geopolitical concepts in the way we manage – is

CONCLUSION – GOOD MANAGEMENT AND SCENARIO PLANNING

needed if we are to master growing complexity both within companies and in the world around us. Yet at the same time, expert knowledge and practical experience are necessary to manage the day-to-day business of our companies.

One piece of good news might help us resolve these contradictions: Corporate management is once again becoming more direct, more personal, more entrepreneurial. It can no longer hide behind models, concepts and techniques. On the contrary, it demands personality, courage, the ability to think and reflect, and a system of proven values. Managers, leaders need to have convictions and take a clear stand. In our view, there are three factors that should influence our definition of good management (Schwenker and Müller-Dofel, 2013):

1. First: Corporate management has become significantly more demanding, as the business environment has also gained complexity. Today's leaders are confronted with uncertainty at every turn. For good management, this means that true entrepreneurial instinct is needed once again as developments become more difficult to predict. It means developing one's own vision for the future and resisting the temptation to follow every trend. It means that it is important for leaders to know where they stand, to be able to make up their own mind about the future and not to go running after every trend that crosses their path. It means that the ability to reflect on things and the willingness to think in interdisciplinary terms is at a premium.

   After all, if we as entrepreneurs want to successfully overcome uncertainty, we need to look beyond our own backyard. We must build bridges to other disciplines. Careful reflection and interdisciplinary thinking don't just materialize out of thin air, however. We must point the training of our managers in this direction, and we must do the same with our day-to-day work.

2. At the same time, we must reassess the tools we use. The traditional strategy and planning concepts that we often hold so dear are not as valid as they once were. And everything that is true for strategy concepts also applies to planning instruments and modern corporate finance methods. We know from experience how exciting it can be to further develop the analytical elegance of a capital asset pricing model. But what is the point of more elegance and precision if the time series of future cashflow is increasingly uncertain?

Today, the words of Albert Einstein are more relevant than ever: "Not everything that can be counted counts, and not everything that counts can be counted." When it comes to good management, this doesn't mean that we should reject the use of modern quantitative models and concepts altogether. Properly applied, these tools can still help reduce complexity and prepare decisions. But we do need to give some serious thought to whether the analytical effort these models require is worthwhile. We should always examine whether we have set the right priorities.

3. When it comes to building trust and giving us a sense of security, what we need is a new understanding of leadership. All of us are looking for security in some form or another. Organizational charts have become a symbol of this longing for security, and of the contradictions that arise from it in these uncertain times. The challenge today is that no truly responsible manager is in a position to say how long any such org chart will remain valid. So we find ourselves in need of something new to replace the security we have lost. As we see it, this can only be anchored in the personality of managers and leaders.

These days, no one can hide behind a number or a plan. Every manager must be able to explain their convictions and how they see the future. To paraphrase Joseph Schumpeter: Those who talk about their visions reveal the limits of their horizons. This is precisely the issue at stake: having a broad horizon – and having the courage to make it known.

8.2
HOW SCENARIO PLANNING SUPPORTS GOOD MANAGEMENT IN UNCERTAIN TIMES

In the uncertain days in which we live, good management is clearly confronted by major challenges. That is precisely where scenario planning comes in – especially our new scenario approach. Scenario planning facilitates good management by tackling several relevant issues at the same time:

◆ Working with scenarios opens the mind. That is true when we are confronted with existing scenarios, but all the more so when we seek to develop scenarios of our own. Start thinking about the future factors that could influence an industry, a

CONCLUSION – GOOD MANAGEMENT AND SCENARIO PLANNING

region or a technology, etc. – perhaps in the context of our new 360° stakeholder feedback process, for example. Start thinking about the uncertainties that surround these influences, their relative weight and how they may be interrelated, and you cannot help but open your mind and broaden your thinking.

♦ Scenario planning improves the quality of business decisions. Our approach to scenario planning targets the key decision levers: It lays a methodological foundation for the implementation of a decision-making process. Especially by bringing together the varying opinions of all relevant stakeholders, it ensures that decision outcomes are less distorted by decision makers' own subjective assessments and perceptions. Above all, it accelerates decision processes by quickly delivering well-founded results and analyses.

♦ Scenario planning gives a company greater strategic flexibility. For example, the impact/uncertainty grid in our scenario approach can help managers assess the influence of market conditions and changes in process variables. Scenario-based planning can also overcome forces of inertia within the organization and break up (or help redirect) well-worn development paths.

♦ Scenarios encourage the interdisciplinary mindset that is essential to good management today. The views of a broad spectrum of stakeholders representing a wide variety of disciplines flow into scenarios. So when managers engage in discussion with marketing experts, economists, engineers and other groups, the picture of the future that emerges is inevitably fuller and more rounded as it is not shaped by a one-sided view.

Other strengths inherent in our new scenario approach are of a more practical nature, but are of equal importance:

♦ Our framing checklist uses three "preplanned" levels of analysis: The micro-level involves scenarios at the level of the business unit or company. The meso-level involves industry scenarios. And the macro-level involves global or regional cross-industry scenarios. This approach enables scenarios to be developed quickly and tailored precisely to specific requirements.

♦ Roland Berger and the HHL Center for Strategy and Scenario Planning have set up a scenario database containing a wealth of high-quality scenario studies (see the website of the HHL Center for Strategy and Scenario Planning: www.scenarioplanning.eu). In scenario projects, we can thus draw on existing scenarios – and again improve both the speed and efficiency of scenario development.

- When planning scenarios, the challenge to management is to pick the right one – and thus to chart the right course from the outset. In our scenario cockpit, monitoring corridors define milestones that indicate when management would do better to switch to a different scenario.

Our firm belief is that good management will have to be able to cope with even greater uncertainty in the future. The HHL and Roland Berger scenario development process outlined in this book is a powerful approach to making robust strategic decisions in an age of uncertainty. While none of us can see into the future, applying the approach described in this book can certainly help prepare us for what lies ahead.

8.3 REFERENCES

Schwenker B., Müller-Dofel M. 2013. *On Good Management. Wiesbaden: Springer Gabler.*

TABLE OF FIGURES

Figure 2.1:	Selected metal prices, 2000-2013 [index, end of Jan 2000 = 100]	25
Figure 2.2:	The New St. Gallen Management Model	34
Figure 3.1:	The HHL-Roland Berger scenario-development process	51
Figure 3.2:	Framing checklist	52
Figure 3.3:	The 360° stakeholder feedback process	54
Figure 3.4:	Blind spot analysis for the electronics retail industry	55
Figure 3.5:	Impact/uncertainty grid for the German long-distance heating industry	57
Figure 3.6:	Scenario matrix for the German long-distance heating industry in 2021	59
Figure 3.7:	Simplified influence diagram for the German long-distance heating industry	60
Figure 3.8:	The scenario-based strategic planning process	63
Figure 4.1:	Six-step scenario-based approach to strategic planning	71
Figure 4.2:	The framing checklist	73
Figure 4.3:	Six-step scenario-based approach to strategic planning	79
Figure 4.4:	360° stakeholder feedback process	81
Figure 4.5:	Scenario planning for European airline network carriers, first-round questionnaire	82
Figure 4.6:	Scenario planning for European airline network carriers, second-round questionnaire	83
Figure 4.7:	Spider diagram of the European airline scenario – Impact: External versus internal view	85
Figure 4.8:	Spider diagram of the European airline scenario – Uncertainty: External versus internal view	86

Figure 4.9:	Second-round questionnaire	93
Figure 4.10:	Blind spots in the impact dimension	94
Figure 4.11:	Blind spots in the uncertainty dimension	95
Figure 4.12:	The six-step scenario-based approach to strategic planning	97
Figure 4.13:	The impact/uncertainty grid	99
Figure 4.14:	The six-step scenario-based approach to strategic planning	101
Figure 4.15:	The scenario matrix	106
Figure 4.16:	The influence diagram	107
Figure 4.17:	Impact/uncertainty grid for the European airline industry	113
Figure 4.18:	Future scenarios for the European airline industry	114
Figure 4.19:	Simplified influence diagram for the European airline industry	115
Figure 4.20:	Scenario fact sheet: Network fortress	118
Figure 4.21:	Scenario fact sheet: Europe under siege	122
Figure 4.22:	Scenario fact sheet: The champions' decline	126
Figure 4.23:	Scenario fact sheet: New horizons	129
Figure 4.24:	The six-step scenario-based approach to strategic planning	131
Figure 4.25:	The strategy corridor	136
Figure 4.26:	The six-step scenario-based approach to strategic planning	138
Figure 4.27:	Influence diagram	140
Figure 4.28:	Indicator table	141
Figure 4.29:	Scenario cockpit: traffic light system	142
Figure 4.30:	Scenarios for the European airline industry	145
Figure 4.31:	Strategy corridor for the European airline industry	146
Figure 4.32:	Influence diagram for the European airline industry	148
Figure 4.33:	Indicator table for the European airline industry	149
Figure 4.34:	Indicator range for the European airline industry (example)	149
Figure 4.35:	Scenario cockpit: traffic light system for the European airline industry	150

TABLE OF FIGURES

Figure 5.1:	The five steps of the scenario process	158
Figure 5.2:	Trends, critical uncertainties and secondary elements within the impact-uncertainty grid	159
Figure 5.3:	Clustering of uncertainties and building of scenarios	160
Figure 5.4:	Spectrum of possible ideas depending on time frame and divergence from core business	170
Figure 6.1:	Integrative model of decision quality	187
Figure 6.2:	Benefits of scenario-based planning	189
Figure 7.1:	Strategic flexibility as a meta-capability	201
Figure 7.2:	Impact of five megatrends on the automotive industry	206
Figure 7.3:	Dimensions of strategic flexibility	208
Figure 7.4:	Impact of the scenario method on lock-ins in strategic planning	210

ABOUT THE EDITORS, AUTHORS AND RBSE

EDITORS

PROF. DR. BURKHARD SCHWENKER
Prof. Dr. Burkhard Schwenker, born 1958, is CEO of Roland Berger Strategy Consultants. From August 2010 to May 2013, he served as Chairman of the international strategy consultancy, a function he took over from the company's founder Prof. Dr. h.c. Roland Berger. As of February 2012, Burkhard Schwenker was also appointed Chairman of the new Roland Berger School of Strategy and Economics (RBSE). He is a regular and acknowledged author in the field of corporate strategy and business policy and teaches strategic management at HHL Leipzig Graduate School of Management. In addition, he volunteers his time to serve as Chairman of the Roland Berger Foundation, Deputy Chairman of Atlantik Brücke e.V. and Chairman of the Board of the Hamburg Symphony Orchestra. He also sits on the Boards of Trustees of the World Wide Fund for Nature (WWF) and the Values Commission (Wertekommission e.V.) and is a member of the Senate of acatech, the German Academy of Science and Engineering.

PROF. DR. TORSTEN WULF
Prof. Dr. Torsten Wulf heads the Chair of Strategic and International Management at Philipps-Universität Marburg. At HHL Leipzig Graduate School of Management, he co-chairs the Center for Strategy and Scenario Planning jointly with Prof. Dr. Burkhard Schwenker. After studying business administration at universities in Mainz and Hagen, he did post-graduate studies at HHL and went on to write a postdoctoral thesis at Friedrich-Alexander-Universität Erlangen-Nürnberg. He was professor for Strategy and International Management at ENPC School of International Management in Paris and regularly teaches as guest professor at business schools and in management training programs in Germany and abroad. His research focuses on behavioral strategy and scenario planning as well as on topics concerning family businesses and top management teams.

AUTHORS

CHRISTIAN BRANDS
Christian Brands studied business administration in Bath and was awarded a Master's degree in Management at HHL Leipzig Graduate School of Management in 2009. Since 2010, he has been doing post-graduate studies at the HHL Center for Strategy and Scenario Planning with Prof. Dr. Torsten Wulf and working as a Research Associate at the Chair for Strategic and International Management at Philipps-Universität Marburg. His research focuses on strategic planning, scenario planning and family businesses.

DR. CORNELIA GEISSLER
Dr. Cornelia Geißler studied economics and sports science at the University of Bayreuth. She received her Ph.D. in 2009, studying under Prof. Dr. Werner Fröhlich (University of Flensburg) and Prof. Dr. Torsten Tomczak (University of St. Gallen). She worked for Handelsblatt Publishing Group, Focus Magazin Verlag and the German edition of the Harvard Business Review. Geißler has been with Roland Berger Strategy Consultants since 2011, most recently working for the Roland Berger School of Strategy and Economics (RBSE). She is an expert in macroeconomic issues, strategic management and scenario planning.

DR. DUCE GOTORA
Dr. Duce Gotora graduated at the University of Oxford with a DPhil in material science. Before joining the Roland Berger Strategy Consultants office in London he worked as a biomedical engineer at Magdi Yacoub Heart Institute. He has more than six years consulting experience in over 30 strategy projects in 12 countries. His expertise ranges from new venture inception to performance improvement. His industry coverage includes oil & gas, consumer goods, energy and chemicals.

NICKLAS HOLGERSSON
Nicklas Holgersson holds a degree in business administration from Georgetown University in Washington, DC, USA. He is a project manager at Roland Berger Strategy Consultants in London and has delivered high-profile international projects

solving strategic and operational issues for senior management of organizations in Europe, North America and South America. Clients include multinational corporations, leading private equity firms, financial institutions and government agencies.

DR. CHRISTIAN KRYS

Dr. Christian Krys studied electrical engineering, business administration and economics at the Ruhr University Bochum and University of Hagen. He received his Ph.D. in 2003 under Prof. Dr. Dodo zu Knyphausen-Aufseß at the University of Bamberg. Krys has been working for Roland Berger Strategy Consultants since 1996 and for the Roland Berger School of Strategy and Economics (RBSE) since 2012. His tasks include managing the Ph.D. program and Academic Network. Krys is an expert in macroeconomic issues, trends and scenario planning.

DR. PHILIP MEISSNER

Dr. Philip Meißner studied business administration in Kiel and gained professional experience in banking and the media industry. In 2008, he completed his MBA studies at HHL Leipzig Graduate School of Management and at Concordia University in Montreal. He did post-graduate studies with Prof. Dr. Torsten Wulf at the Center for Strategy and Scenario Planning and contributed to building the Center after its foundation in 2009. Since 2012, Meißner has been writing a post-doctoral thesis at Philipps-Universität Marburg. His research focuses on strategic decision-making processes, behavioral strategy and scenario planning.

DR. STEPHAN STUBNER

Dr. Stephan Stubner heads the Chair of Strategic Management and Family Business at HHL Leipzig Graduate School of Management. He studied in Paderborn, Phoenix, Granada and Leipzig and received his doctorate from Friedrich-Alexander-Universität Erlangen-Nürnberg. Before embarking on his career in academia, he gained entrepreneurial experience as the founder and CEO of two companies and as a strategy consultant. His research focus is on strategy and scenario planning, family businesses and entrepreneurship.

ABOUT RBSE

EXCELLENCE IN RESEARCH AND TEACHING

Roland Berger School of Strategy and Economics (RBSE) is the new corporate university of Roland Berger Strategy Consultants. It is where our consultants pool their knowledge, and the means by which they share it both within Roland Berger and with the outside world. We ensure hands-on knowledge transfer through high-quality courses, soon available to clients and business partners too. Our publications present the latest research findings and a unique store of methodological expertise.

RBSE's mission is to help business leaders master the complexities of corporate management and develop sustainable strategies. To achieve this mission, we analyze the latest trends in business and society and investigate their impact on the corporate community. In THOUGHTS, our series of publications for thought leaders, we provide a cross-industry and interdisciplinary angle on key issues that shape the future. RBSE collaborates closely with a global network of first-class academics to deliver on its promise of excellence in research and teaching.

www.rolandberger.com/rbse
rbse@rolandberger.com

CPSIA information can be obtained
at www.ICGtesting.com
Printed in the USA
FFOW03n1318180416
23349FF